BOARDROOM
BULLRIDER

BOARDROOM BULLRIDER

BRYAN F. MERRITT

BULLRIDER PRESS
Firestone, Colorado
2018

Bryan F. Merritt is a 20-year Senior Executive, Executive Coach, and Business Development Leader. In 1999, he founded Matrix Management Systems, LLC a Contract Executive firm focused on providing strategic, executive level management to companies in financial distress.

 Download the accompanying workbook from the *Boardroom Bullrider* website at BoardroomBullrider.com

Contact the Boardroom Bullrider to coach/facilitate the implementation of your organization's next key initiative or to speak at an upcoming event. For consulting services contact *BoardroomBullrider@gmail.com*

Published, May 2018
© 2016 by Matrix Management Systems, LLC

ISBN
978-1-5323-6096-1   Paperback

Distributed by Matrix Management Systems, LLC
Firestone, Colorado

Shutterstock photos on pages —
x, xiv, xvii, xxiii, xxxii, xxxiv, 10, 36, 60, 65, 82, 88, 108, 140, 153-156.
Frog Illustrationpg 143—Zack Christian ©2018
Wholesale and quantity discounts available upon request.
BoardroomBullrider.com

ART DIRECTION, BOOK DESIGN
© 2017. All Rights Reserved by
 A. J. Business Design & Publishing Center Inc.
home of the award-winning Tendril Press publishing house
AJImagesinc.com—TendrilPress.com—303•696•9227
Info@AJImagesInc.com—publisher@TendrilPress.com

Boardroom Bullrider is dedicated to those past clients who awarded me the privilege of working together through some of their most difficult business issues. Their patience and dedication to the process, coupled with their willingness to do the work, produced some amazing results.

There is more to running a business
than just owning a suit and
there's more to being a cowboy
than just wearing the boots.

Contents

CHARTS AND ILLUSTRATIONS

BULL RIDING TERMS

Arena–The arena is the fenced in area where the bull-riding event takes place. Typically averages 85 feet by 140 feet.

Away from His Hand–Bull riders use the term "away from his hand" to describe the scenario where a bull is spinning in the direction opposite a rider's riding hand.

Back Pens–A maze of steel panels located behind the bucking chutes and connected together, creating pens that serve as a holding and loading area for the bulls awaiting their turn.

Barrel Man–The barrel man works in the center of the arena with a custom-made barrel that protects him from a charging bull and provides the bull riders an island of safety if they are bucked off far from the arena fence or bucking chutes.

Buckle–The winning bull rider is normally presented with the sport's coveted silver buckle, the symbolic trophy for winning the event.

Bucking Chute–Each bull is loaded into a gated steel box called a chute. The bull rider and bull remain in the chute until the rider is ready. He nods his head, signaling the gate man to open the gate and allow the ride to begin.

Bull Rope–The bull rope is wrapped around the chest of the bull directly behind the animal's front legs, giving the bull rider something to hold onto throughout the ride. At the bottom of the rope hangs a metal bell designed to pull the rope off as soon as the rider is bucked off or dismounts the animal.

Bullfighter—A bullfighter or clown's job is to distract a bull when a rider bucks off before or after the eight seconds, giving the rider a chance to get back to his feet and out of harm's way.

Buzzer—A buzzer is sounded when the bull rider has ridden the bull for the required 8 seconds. He is free to get off the bull once the buzzer sounds indicating a successful ride.

Cover—When a rider "covers" his bull, he successfully remains on the bull for eight seconds and therefore earns a score from the judges.

Dismount—To dismount, a bull rider reaches down with his free hand, pulls on the tail of the rope to free his riding hand, and flings himself off while the bull is still bucking. The momentum will usually propel the rider away from the bull.

Disqualified—A bull rider is disqualified if he touches the bull or himself with his free hand or if his riding hand comes out of the bull rope at any point during the eight-second ride.

Down in the Well—The expression "down in the well" is a situation in which a bull is spinning in one direction and the force of the spin pulls the rider down the side of the bull into the vortex, often resulting in a bull rider getting hung up on the bull.

Draw—An event's list of bulls and the riders randomly selected to ride them is called the "draw." If a bull rider says he has a "good draw," it means he was paired with a bull that he wanted to ride.

Eight Seconds—Eight seconds is the amount of time a bull rider must stay on his bull with his hand in the rope to receive a score.

Flank Strap—A flank strap is a strap that goes around the flank of a bull. Its purpose is to encourage the bull to kick its hind legs high in the air when trying to get the rider off. The flank strap never goes around a bull's genitals, and no sharp objects are ever placed inside the flank strap that could potentially hurt the animal.

Gate Man—A gate man is located inside the arena in front of the chute from which a ride is about to start. The gate man holds onto a rope tied to the designated chute's gate, awaiting the bull rider's cue to open the chute gate and allow the ride to begin.

Hooked—When a bull rider is bucked off, the bull sometimes goes after the rider or the bullfighter, attempting to hook or stab them with his horns. This is known as being "hooked."

Hung up—Sometimes a rider gets thrown from a bull but his riding hand remains in his bull rope; therefore, the rider is "hung up" on the bull. When this happens, bullfighters quickly move in to help the bull rider free his hand and get away from the bull.

Into his Hand—Bull riders use the term "into his hand" to describe a bull spinning in the same direction of the rider's hand in the rope. Example: the bull rider is holding onto the rope with his right hand, and the bull is spinning to the right.

Rank—A bull that is difficult to ride is considered "rank."

Rowels—The sharp, star-shaped object mounted at the end of a spur. This star or rowel, when pushed into the bull's side, helps the rider's feet stay down, assisting him in staying on the bull. The use of these rowels does not hurt or cut the bull's hide.

Rosin—A natural, chalky substance that a bull rider rubs onto the hand-hold area of his bull rope and riding glove. Rosin makes the rope and riding glove extremely sticky, aiding his ability to hold onto the rope during the ride.

Slap—If a rider touches the bull or himself with his free hand during a ride, it is called a slap. He is disqualified and does not receive a score.

Spinner—A bull that is bucking in a spinning pattern throughout the ride is often referred to by bull riders as a "spinner."

Spurs—Bull riders wear spurs that have dull, loosely locked rowels (the wheel-like part of the spur). The spurs help a rider maintain his balance, giving him added grip with his feet. The dull spurs do not cut or scratch a bull's hide.

ACKNOWLEDGEMENTS

I would like to acknowledge several individuals and organizations, in addition to those quoted in the book, that have provided personal time, papers, articles, and books that have contributed to the work of *Boardroom Bullrider.*

Special thanks go to Lin Tiffany for her countless hours of reading draft after draft. Her contributions as chief editor have significantly improved the content of this work. Thank you for the words of encouragement over the years.

Thanks to my good friend John K. Sawyer for his early contributions in helping me get my initial ideas conceptualized and on paper.

I want to recognize Kelly Newcomb, who helped develop many of the concepts and ideas included in this book. Our relentless debates regarding the material have insured the processes taught in this work are relevant to any business climate.

My kids, Brian and Hailey McMillan and Mallory Hutchins, provided help with editing, photo design, and layout. It has been great to have them close and willing to jump in when needed.

Finally, my wife Diane has supported me through a very difficult time when I probably needed to be doing other things. Her inspiration regarding the value of *Boardroom Bullrider* has provided the motivation needed to complete the work.

Thanks, and I love you all!

There is nothing worse
than wasted potential. —

How It All Began

My grandfather was a cattle rancher in Star Valley, Wyoming. Working on a cattle ranch requires hard work and long days. I spent many a summer as a young boy working on that ranch.

Every spring we would have a cattle drive, taking the cattle to the summer range high in the Wyoming mountains. I was six years old, riding an old buckskin mare named "Old Goldie." Dressed in blue jeans and an old hat, with my lunch packed carefully by my grandmother and tucked neatly in my saddle bag, I would head off with my grandfather just as the sun was breaking over the mountain peaks for a long day of "pushin' cattle."

My grandfather had a timeworn rodeo arena on the summer range. During these spring cattle drives, this arena was used for branding and vaccinating the young cattle. It was hot and dirty work. One-by-one, we would hold the young calves down for my grandfather. The smell from the hot branding iron as it made its mark hung thick in the air.

In that small arena, we actually had our own buckaroo rodeo. My uncles would have some fun trying to ride the bigger steers while my brother and I would watch intently and pretend that someday we too would be bull riders.

I rode Old Goldie and chased the cattle all summer, mostly for the fun of it. In the fall, we would round the cattle up and drive them back down to the homestead for the winter. As I grew into a teenager, the cowboy life never wore off. I still enjoyed riding horses, roping steers, and working around cattle.

Each year, we'd celebrate the 4th of July by going to one of the regional rodeos. The best one, as I recall, was held in Jackson Hole, Wyoming. I would watch the bucking horses and bulls in amazement. I wondered how on earth those cowboys could stay on those bucking animals. My favorite event was the last event—bull-riding. It is always the event's grand finale.

The bulls were big and mean. As the workers pushed the bulls into the chutes, my heart raced with excitement. The cowboys would try their best to ride for 8 seconds with most ending up getting slammed to the dirt.

The rodeo clowns were fearless. They worked to keep the bulls away from the riders by running right in front of the bull, making themselves an easy target. This would distract the bull long enough for the rider to escape. Bull-riding is fast and furious action that many times results in cowboys being carried out of the arena on a stretcher.

Make no mistake—bull-riding is definitely a world-class sport and without question the most dangerous sport on earth. It requires a balance of ruggedness and finesse and the ability to look fear in the eyes without flinching. These bull riders are gutsy athletes.

I never really thought about actually *riding* a bull myself. Then I turned sixteen, and, like most sixteen-year-old boys, I thought I was invincible. I decided I would give it a try.

People, my friends and family for sure, thought I was crazy. Maybe it was a good dose of peer pressure as well, but I simply couldn't get the thought of riding a bull out of my head. It really didn't seem all that dangerous.

Now, you need to understand that bull-riding's not the kind of sport where one can get a whole lot of practice. It's not like you can just go to a gym. I didn't really know what I was getting myself into. Oh sure, I could watch and see what other riders did to prepare and how they rode their bulls. But I couldn't experience the real thing. I wouldn't be able to truly understand bull-riding until I rode a bull myself.

My First Ride

My first bull ride was a PRCA (Pro Rodeo Cowboys Association) sanctioned event held on July 4, 1975, at the Rexburg, Idaho, 4th of July Celebration Parade and Rodeo. I paid a $25 fee to ride since I was not an official member. In 1975, $25 was a lot of money to a sixteen-year-old living a cowboy lifestyle.

My parents didn't seem to mind at all when I told them the news. Maybe I should have questioned their eagerness for me to give it a try. I guess they thought I was going through a phase. I would give it a try and forget about it. I wouldn't last the 8 seconds, one and done.

In advance of the event, I sent in my waiver and release form, paid my fee, and spent the next two weeks psyching myself out, which in reality meant I was scared to death. I walked around with my chest out, boasting, having made the decision to get on my first bull. Somehow, I thought it would help calm me down a bit. It didn't work.

The truth of the matter was I still had no idea what I was doing. I had no equipment. No hat, no rope, nothing. For this first ride I had to borrow it all. Well, all except for the hat—you can't borrow someone else's hat, bad karma. I bought a used hat for five dollars from a friend a few days before the competition. It was white and well-worn with a slight sweat ring showing through. It made me look like the real thing!

To prepare for my first ride, I went to my friends' house where we'd practice. They had an old bucking barrel, a 55-gallon drum hung on its side,

Char's Rodeo Practice Bucking Barrel —Seniors Walking Across America

strung up between three poles with ropes, which I would find out later is nothing like riding a real bull. We each took our turn getting on the barrel while the others would pull down hard on the ropes.

If nothing else, I learned how it felt to hit the dirt. We spent hours riding that barrel, talking about bulls, and getting ready to ride.

In the days leading up the ride, I received all kinds of sage advice, lots of ideas, plenty of people telling me what to expect. Because I had no actual experience in the arena, other than that old barrel, very little of it made much sense to me.

I tried to imagine the bull and to visualize myself riding him. To feel the speed and power of the first turn out of the gate. To hear the roar of the crowd as the bull and I did battle in the arena.

From the practice barrel, I knew I'd ride left-handed, meaning I'd grip the rope with my left hand and leave my right arm free in an attempt to keep my balance. I had no sense of what balance even meant because I'd never *been* on the back of a bull before. I assured myself it would be the same as a horse. I knew horses.

The day of the Rexburg Rodeo finally came. Wearing my well-worn five-dollar hat, I took it all in. I recall the smell of the bulls and the distinct odor of rosin, the hard, sticky substance riders rubbed into their bull ropes and gloves to get them to stick tightly together.

I watched intently as each rider got physically and mentally prepared, hoping to catch a few last-minute tips. Even then, I didn't grasp the full extent of what was going on with these riders and all their curious pre-ride rituals. But I let the excitement behind the chutes seep into me.

Cowboys on deck visualize, build courage, manage their anticipation. They're wrestling within their mind to answer, "How am I going to ride this bull for 8 seconds? What do I need to do to be in just the right place doing precisely the right thing when that bull and I are two, three, four seconds into the ride? When the bull does what I don't expect, what counter-move will I need to make to get to the buzzer and the coveted 8 seconds?"

At the same time, they're trying to push out of their mind what happened to the last rider who made an attempt to ride this bull. Maybe he got bucked off quickly or, even worse, got stepped on. Bull riders can't focus on the negative; they have to focus on the positive. They must visualize themselves making the ride and getting to the 8-second buzzer.

I walked around behind the chutes like I was a bull-riding veteran. Unless you were riding in the event, you weren't allowed back there. But I *was* there. I was a bull rider!

Seemed like that evening dragged on forever. Hours went by. I knew beforehand which bull I'd be riding, when my turn would come up, and which chute I'd come out of. I had so much extra time to think, I nearly talked myself out of it. The fear just sat there, festering in the pit of my stomach like sour milk.

I watched the bronc riders, the calf-roping, the bareback horses, and the steer wrestling. During the barrel-racing event, I always had to have a cheeseburger. There is something about eating a cheeseburger at the rodeo, and when the barrel-racing started, it just seemed like the perfect time.

Rodeo was in the air. The big arena lights were turned on as the night came. You could see the dust hanging in the air as you looked across the arena toward the grandstand.

Then it happened, the moment I was waiting for. It was time for the grand finale, the final event, bull-riding! The announcer made the call. My heart began pounding in my chest.

Big John–The Competition

To pair a cowboy with a bull, the name of the bull is written on a list and the rider's name is drawn from a hat. It's all done by random selection. The draw had paired me to ride a two-thousand-pound Black Angus bull named "Big John." While hanging out behind the chutes, I went to the holding pens to size up Big John. I climbed on the fence and looked over the top for a better view.

Let's just say that Big John was—BIG!

When there is a fence between you and a bull and he's over there milling around, he's just a bull. He's not that big, he's just standing there, and he's not riled up (yet). His eyes look down at the ground and his tail shuffles left and right, swatting at flies. He's just a stupid bull. He's no threat whatsoever. He seems so friendly.

But when they bring that bull around and put him in that small, tight chute, the whole picture changes. Up close the bulls are *huge*. It's not about having a clear head anymore; your body is starting to talk to you. And it speaks the language of fear.

Now you're looking down at that bull. He's close enough for you to touch him. All the negative voices talking in your head are screaming now: *Are you sure you're really gonna do this? You think this'll be fun? Look at the size of those horns!*

The intimidation factor goes up tenfold the closer you get to show time. This was the first time I'd actually sat on a bucking bull. The bull I saw resting in the holding pens now felt twice the size, like a fire-breathing dragon waiting to slay the brave knight.

For whatever reason, once you see your bull up close, the butterflies in your stomach turn to vultures. It becomes almost impossible to keep your focus. Your hands are wringing with sweat. Your mind tells you you're ready, but your body is expressing the silent shakes of defiant disagreement. That feeling, that's your body talking—that's what fear and intimidation feel like to a bull rider.

Late in the event, the chute boss finally called my name. Big John and I were up. I grabbed my borrowed equipment, went down to my assigned bucking chute, and up onto the chute rail I climbed. Crouched above Big John now, I gracefully eased myself down onto his back. I had to keep my knees high because of the extremely tight quarters in the bucking chute.

The chute workers had set my rope earlier, and now they handed the tail of the rope to me. I slid my hand into the braided hand-hold and tried to act as if I had done this a thousand times. I told myself, *you can do this!*

I soon learned that sliding down on the bull was the easy part. The scene quickly became chaotic in my effort to get settled, to get my rope situated just right—wherever just right was. Then came the question of how tight to pull the rope. I took just a second longer to try to figure out how to sit on this thing. Adrenaline must have been blowing out my ears.

I came to the chutes thinking the back of a bull would be somewhat wide and flat, but when you sit your butt down on a bull, what you feel is backbone. What you're sitting upon is like a fence rail that's about to come to life. I couldn't help but think, "This massive rail-of-a-thing's about ready to bolt out of there and spin and buck, kick and jump, and go in all different directions—with me on it!"

From the get-go, Big John was trying to get me off his back. If you're starting to slide down to the right, he's gonna lean to the left. Too far back, he will jump forward. Too far forward, he will back out from under you. He wants nothing more than to get you off his back.

As soon as my weight rested on Big John's back, he lunged forward. I was thrown hard toward the front of the chute like a truck had slammed into the back of me. Immediately, the chute boss barked at me to get my spurs out of the bull's sides. "Keep your toes pointed in boy! Or that bull is gonna kill ya!"

Bull riders wear spurs with rowels that point inward from their heels to help keep their feet down while the bull is bucking. If you don't keep your toes pointed in, the spurs jab into the bull's sides. He will lean hard and jump around, and you'll never get out of the chute if you're irritating him that way.

There isn't much room in there. Your legs are hanging down between the bull and the rails of the chute. A two-thousand-pound bull could snap a leg without much effort. I heeded the chute boss's advice.

I pressed my hand into the center of the bull's back, felt his breath squeezing in and out of him. His heart pounded—or was that mine? Tied to the back of Big John, he and I were one. I was in the zone, barely aware of the roar of the crowd, totally focused. My mind was saying, *Heck yeah! You can do this!*

The handlers cinched up the bull rope and told me, "You gotta tighten that rope, boy! Get 'er real tight now." I had no idea how tight "real tight" was. It felt too tight already! I couldn't even close my hand around it.

The rope was hot and sticky from all the rosining I'd done. I tried to move my hand a bit to loosen the death grip of the rope, but it didn't help. Big John was ready to get out of that chute. He was leaning hard against the gate and my knee was pinned in-between. As Big John moved, jostled and breathed, his massive body expanded, keeping the rope constricted around my hand.

I wrapped the tail of the rope around my gloved hand as I had been shown, and that pulled everything tighter. Big John was throwing his head up and down as if he was losing patience—like he knew this was my first ride. I slid up on my rope, which nestled my fist deep into my crotch. I was practically sitting on my knuckles. Let's just say it felt awkward, but I was doing what everybody had told me to do.

The blood circulation to my hand, the one in the rope, was now cut off ,and I was sitting there with my fist deep into my crotch. I thought, *this can't be right*. I just wanted to *survive* this ride. I wanted to save face among the bull riders, to show them I was up to the challenge.

With my right hand, I pushed my five-dollar hat down tight. The gateman was looking for the nod from me to go. Every muscle in my body instantly went tight. I nodded my head. That's when I heard it—the latch on the chute gate snapped back. The big wooden gate swung open.

Of course, Big John heard this too, and to a bucking bull, that sound triggers the craziness to begin. The chute always opens from the bulls' backside; otherwise, the fence would hit the riders as they left the chute. This forces the bull to turn sideways in order to enter the arena straightaway.

The gatemen pulled that big gate open wide as fast and hard as he could. As the gate swung to the right, Big John entered the arena with me on his back, holding on for dear life. I leaned forward out over his head to get past the first jump.

Big John did not like me on his back. To make matters worse, the chute boss gave him one last shot on the rump with a cattle prod. My head was jerked back hard as he blew out of the chute. The force slid my body back, and I hit the end of my arm gripping at the rope. Big John made his first hard turn in an attempt to hook my leg with his horn.

As I left the chutes, I heard my buddies hollering, "Feet! Feet!" At this point you have to turn your toes out, driving your spurred heels into the sides of the bull. If you don't, your feet will fly out, and it's all but over.

I most certainly wasn't prepared for anything so strong. It's akin to a twisting, twirling, out-of-control amusement park ride with no safety harness. But by now I was past the point of no return.

My arm was jerked hard as the weight of my body moved quickly backward. Pulling on the rope in a frantic effort to catch up, I gripped it with all the strength I could muster. With my free hand high in the air, I did my best to keep upright on the back of this train wreck.

My feet flew outward from the force as my body was jerked toward the back of the bull. I was trying as hard as I could to get back into position. I could hear the roar of the crowd saying, "Keep riding! Keep riding!"

Everything slipped into slow motion. I was using every muscle in my body as I attempted to stay on top of this massive bull. Nothing could have prepared me for this wild ride.

I felt my hand come out of the rope, something a few seconds earlier I thought could never happen. Suddenly, there was air under my butt, and it felt as if I was hanging in midair. I landed hard on my back, slamming my head into the dirt. My ears were ringing, and I couldn't catch my breath. It all happened so fast!

Big John won! He bucked me off after two or three hard lunges. I remember seeing him going in the other direction and realizing I was on the ground, but still alive. My mouth was full of dirt, and all I could think about was getting up and out of the arena.

Then I heard the buzzer from the judge's booth and knew there was no way I'd made it anywhere close to the prized 8 seconds—maybe two or three, if even that.

My well-worn five-dollar hat was still on my head though, even after flying through the air and getting slammed to the dirt. The rodeo clowns were now between me and Big John. I got to my feet, ran back to the chutes, and climbed over the fence.

I Was a Bull Rider!

"Atta boy!" My cowboy compadres were applauding and congratulating me for having made my first ride. At the same time, they recalled the ride for me jump for jump. "The first jump was great; you looked smooth. Second jump, you lost your feet. You have to keep your feet down. Stay up on the rope. You got behind and slid back. Too much force on your arm. Your dismount was a real crowd pleaser though." Yeah, that sounded about right.

Everybody was slapping me on the back. That's when I knew I was hooked. I knew this wasn't a one-time thing. I knew I was going to do this again and again. I brushed the dirt off of my now "bull-riding" hat and put it back on my head, cocked just a little to one side.

I spent the rest of the night acting like a pro, working the chutes, helping the other bull riders get on, and giving advice. That day I became a bull rider.

I was determined to conquer this sport. I fell in love with the challenge, probably because it was just so much harder than one could ever imagine.

The power and speed of that bull was unbelievable. I had never experienced anything like it.

The preparation. The adrenaline. The rush. The thrill. The friendship. The rodeo life was exciting, dangerous, and captivating. Thus began my lifelong love affair with the sport of bull-riding.

Big John? I probably rode him for two or three seconds, but he gave me a lifetime of guidance. I vividly remember that July 4th Rodeo in Rexburg, Idaho. It's a memory, a time-stamped experience, that's forever in my mind. In many ways, it shaped me into who I am today.

Bull-Riding and Business

Today I'm a husband, a father, and a grandfather. In my professional career, I'm a contract executive. I fix things, drawing on a variety of skills I've honed—from leadership coaching to corporate turnarounds. As I leave every morning to go to work in my business attire, my bull rope, chaps and spurs hang on a hat rack in my den as a reminder of my younger days.

When I tell business colleagues that I used to ride bulls, they stare at me in amazement. They say, "What were you thinking? You must have been crazy!" I believe it gives them a different perspective of me, perhaps some added confidence that I am decisive, courageous, and a no-nonsense business leader.

Their reaction in turn gives me renewed confidence. I take pride in the fact that I had an opportunity in my life to do something that most folks wouldn't do. Especially something requiring such a high level of courage and determination.

I find myself reflecting on those memories of my bull-riding days, a spot deep inside me that reminds me I truly can achieve anything I put my mind to. You know—the place in your gut that says, *bring it on!*

Bull-riding is not easy. It takes a lot of practice. Building a successful business isn't easy either. It takes hard work. In both cases, you have to step into the arena and take a risk, then another, and another. Each time, you push your fear aside, act, and learn. Win or lose, you learn.

Today, the business environment is competitive and difficult. Yet, plenty of room exists for fundamental, no-nonsense improvement. And by that, I mean the kind of improvement that takes guts. Tough decisions. Decisive action.

I learned from bull-riding to take each day as a challenge to work hard, focusing on what's required to succeed, and to create something of value. Once you have it, you have to fight to keep it. You have to stand strong and deliver. Pay the price.

When a bull rider ties his hand in the rope and nods for the gate, *that's commitment!* That's making a tough decision and seeing it through. That's a decision made in spite of the intimidation and the danger of being on top of a bull he can't control. The rider knows the possible outcomes. Remember, even if the rider is successful and makes the 8 seconds, there's only one way off. You have to land in the dirt.

In life and in business, you most certainly have to make hard decisions. You most certainly will land in the dirt. Those of you with guts will pick yourselves up and keep going. You will find success in your arena if you are disciplined enough to work hard, push aside your fears, and keep moving forward.

Marketplace uncertainty is something we cannot control. Companies cannot achieve longstanding viability without managing through the difficulties. The point of this book is to give you the tools necessary to navigate through the difficult times and then to celebrate your success.

You must see what you want and go get it, to not be intimidated when it gets tough, to stay focused on the prize, to build lasting friendships along the way, and to leave behind a great legacy.

Looking back, I learned everything I needed to know about success in 8 seconds. Are you ready? Well, then, rosin up, tighten your rope, pull your hat down, point your toes out, and nod your head for the ride of your life!

Go ahead…Get on!

Grab the bull rope and nod for the gate.
See how much you can learn in 8 seconds!

BOARDROOM BULLRIDER

INTRODUCTION

It takes guts to tie your hand to the back of a bucking bull, nod your head, and turn him loose into the arena. My bull-riding days are long gone now; it's a young man's sport. Even so, my pulse quickens as I sit in the grandstands, wearing my boots and black bull-riding hat, watching today's young bull riders as they bear down and nod for the gate.

As I watch the bulls explode out of the chute, my muscles flex, remembering the intensity. My body tics and twitches as my mind unconsciously makes the adjustments needed to make the ride. In my mind, I still see every counter-move as the cowboys try to make the 8-second buzzer. My anxiety peaks as the rider gets slammed to the dirt, the clowns working to assist his escape. I slide to the edge of my seat until the rider safely exits the arena.

My career as a business executive has taken me out of the bull-riding arena to the lavish environment of boardrooms around the world, developing strategic plans, identifying next-level opportunities, and skillfully implementing those plans to achieve financial success. From Seoul to San Francisco and from Venice to Vancouver, I've visited scores of countries and every state in these United States. But in my heart, I'm still a cocky sixteen-year-old bull rider from Idaho.

It likewise takes guts to show up, step into the competitive business arena, and take control of a company when others are out of ideas and ready to give up. Business turnarounds have been my expertise for most of my career. I've witnessed amazing moments of strength as a leader steps up to achieve the impossible. I was once asked, "Why do you do it?" I responded, "Because I can!"

Boardroom Bullrider will teach you how to quickly identify the problem, construct the go-forward strategy, hone the organizational focus, and get the business back on track. It will give you the confidence to eliminate the roadblocks and to develop key relationships that matter. And, as I have discovered, the five lessons covered in this book will take you wherever you want to go.

Let me teach you how I found the inner strength to be a bull rider. Let me use that to teach you how to find *your* inner strength—the strength needed to succeed in your own arena!

The title of this book, *Boardroom Bullrider*, consists of two metaphors. The first metaphor is that of a boardroom, where the giants of business are on stage. This image represents my career in business. My experiences span a 30-year period of working with a diverse array of companies, each with its own unique opportunities and challenges.

The second metaphor is that of a bull rider in the arena where the giants of rodeo are on stage. This image represents the one single event that had such an impact on my life that it can never be forgotten. I was in fact a bull rider and the images, feelings, emotions, and fears experienced during those years can be recalled as if it were yesterday.

Put them together, *Boardroom Bullrider*, and you have a no-nonsense approach to getting and keeping your business on track. My experiences as a bull rider, coupled with the lessons I've learned restoring troubled companies to profitability, provide the backdrop for this work.

As you experience my story and what I have learned from it, I encourage you to inject your own metaphors. Discover the single event that changed your life. Maybe it hasn't happened yet. This book will inspire you to create a vision for yourself and encourage you to make it a reality.

The 5 Lessons I Learned In 8 Seconds:

1. **Thinking**—What was I thinking? What on earth possessed me to get on a bull in the first place? I explore the ways we think when called upon to make tough decisions. The objective of Lesson One is to teach you how to practice balanced-thinking to **Create a Compelling Vision.**

   Create a Compelling Vision—Ability to clearly form mental images of things or events, i.e., identify processes, procedures, goals, targets, potential complications, and probable solutions.

2. **Intimidation**—There's nothing more intimidating than getting on the back of a bull. We have all experienced intimidation at various points in our lives. Lesson Two will teach you how to identify and **Eliminate Your Intimidators.** When you take a step forward and do the most-right thing now, you can get past the intimidators standing between you and your goals.

   Eliminate your Intimidators—Possess strong, dedicated, and focused leadership qualities, positioning oneself clearly in front of the organization, reinforcing the vision, and modeling the way.

3. **Balance**—It takes a great deal of balance to stay atop a bucking bull for 8 long seconds. You must focus intently on the task at hand. Getting slammed to the arena floor is the result when you lose focus. Lesson Three will walk you through the required steps to identify and **Focus on the Critical Issues** that cause you to lose momentum.

   Focus on the Critical Issues—The ability to execute a plan, idea, model, design, specification, standard, or policy while at the same time identifying and eliminating any or all constraints.

4. **Clowns**—A bull rider's best friend. Without the help of clowns, a bull rider would be an easy target. Clowns risk their lives by distracting the bull, allowing just enough time for the rider to get out of the arena. Who are the clowns in your life, standing ready to assist you in achieving your vision? Lesson Four discusses how you **Develop Key Relationships** with those individuals who are critical to your success.

Develop Key Relationships—Understand the importance of relationships and that companies don't make decisions, people do. People do business with people they know, like, and trust.

5. **Self-preservation**—Bull-riding is an extremely dangerous sport. Sometimes, things don't go as planned, and you and the bull engage in the contest of your life. During those moments when you find yourself in peril, your self-preservation mode kicks in, and you perform feats well beyond your normal capabilities. Outside the arena, self-preservation can turn into selfish-preservation. If you want to build strong teams and sustainable processes that deliver, remember: it's not about you. Lesson Five will encourage you to shift attention away from yourself and onto the processes that create value and are required to **Build a Sustainable Organization.**

Build a Sustainable Organization—Provide a path or process to enlarge, develop, or expand beyond the current state in a positive, sustainable direction with processes that minimize defects and deliver value.

What and How

Each of the five *Boardroom Bullrider* lessons encompasses the "**What**" factor. **What** is needed to effect positive change. **What** is needed to implement a strategic plan. **What** is needed to achieve financial success. And **What** is needed to sustain growth.

At the end of each lesson is the "**How**" factor titled "**Getting on the Bull.**" It provides the instruction and training on the aptitudes necessary to master the five lessons. **How** do you effect positive change? **How** do you implement a strategic plan? **How** do you achieve financial stability? And **how** do you sustain growth?

Take the time to read and consider each aptitude before moving on. There is a progression here. When you do the work, it will have a significant impact, propelling you toward your vision. Make sure your vision and goals are developed by using balanced-thinking. Write your vision down, and continue to work with it through the next four lessons and their following workshops.

Having worked in and with troubled companies, I've observed all of them struggling with the same obvious issue: the lack of profitability. These companies were working hard but simply not producing enough cash to sustain their operations.

As we worked together to return these companies to profitability, I discovered the same five basic issues were the root cause of their troubles. By simply teaching these organizations how to employ the five lessons from *Boardroom Bullrider*, I helped them to quickly return to profitability, in many cases exceeding their expectations.

Their employees became re-engaged in the business. Goals were achieved and celebrated. Most important, they learned how to sustain their newfound success.

Once you incorporate the five lessons, you will build a thriving organization. First, though, you have to admit that you could be, in fact, doing better—and then get started doing the necessary work.

One of my clients responded with "I didn't know we were broken! I only wish we had met you sooner!"

Don't be that guy! Don't ignore the subtle indicators of trouble. Don't spend your valuable time working IN your business and put off working ON your business. When we ignore the problems, they only get worse.

Unfortunately, the five lessons aren't radical and new. I'm sure you have read similar books, possibly even tried implementing similar ideas like these dozens of times. The significant difference in the *Boardroom Bullrider* lessons is the added attention to focus. *You will quickly learn that by separating the critical few from the trivial many, you get sustainable results.*

Bull-Riding

The photograph on the top of the next page is of me riding a bull for the coveted 8 seconds at the Lincoln County Fair and Rodeo in Afton, Wyoming. The year was 1977, and I was eighteen years old. By then, I had been riding bulls for about two years. I can still vividly remember that ride. I actually made a ride on a bull that was good enough to win.

There is a saying in bull-riding: "If you draw a bull rank enough to win on, you can't ride him; if you draw a bull rank enough to ride, you can't win on him!"

I can still to this day remember the sights, sounds, and smells of that moment. It has burned an indelible memory I have carried with me throughout my life. However, it wasn't until later in my career that I made the connection.

Spirit of '76, Lincoln County Fair — Payne Photography

I had been working as a business consultant with companies in turn-around situations. I was involved with one particular business that was in an extremely serious financial condition. As I worked to develop the strategy that would eventually return this company to profitability, I found myself connecting with those earlier memories and that 8-second ride.

I made the connection between what it takes to make an 8-second ride on the back of a raging bull and what was missing from this company. As a result, the lack of employing these five lessons had driven them into financial trouble. More important, I realized the five lessons would get this company back on track.

It doesn't matter which functional area of the organization you work in or are concerned about; all require the same five lessons for success. While working as a sales professional, I learned my success was clearly dependent on mastering these five lessons. In later management assignments, I discovered the required aptitudes were the same.

I have included five, one-page pre-assessments at the beginning of each lesson to measure your current effectiveness. These pre-assessments will help you to identify where you are and where you might need to focus.

Take the opportunity to identify your organization's *ONE CRITICAL* Strength, Weakness, Opportunity, and Threat (CRITICAL SWOT) measured against these five disciplines and their respective aptitudes. This is your first opportunity to practice focus. Go ahead and make a list, writing them all down; but before you move on, identify the ONE in each SWOT category that is "most" important.

Capture your thoughts as you review the pre-assessment results. This will help you organize them as you discover the five lessons of *Boardroom Bullrider*.

BOARDROOM BULLRIDER

LESSON 1

THINKING
CREATE A COMPELLING VISION

Thinking—What was I thinking? What on earth possessed me to get on a bull in the first place? I explore the ways we think when called upon to make tough decisions. The objective of Lesson One is to teach you how to practice balanced-thinking when **Creating a Compelling Vision.**

Create a Compelling Vision—Ability to clearly form mental images of things or events, i.e., identify processes, procedures, goals, targets, potential complications, and probable solutions.

PRE-ASSESSMENT: CREATE A COMPELLING VISION

❑ You have a financial budgeting process for the current financial year.

❑ You possess the ability to measure, review, and adjust to meet the current targets.

❑ There is cross-functional development of organizational targets and goals.

❑ The employees are aware of the stated objectives, and they measure them.

❑ There is a clean transition in direction from management down through the organization.

❑ There are incentives (nonfinancial) in place to celebrate success.

The Strength: _____

The Weakness: _____

The Opportunity: _____

The Threat: _____

You simply can't react
your way to a goal. —

I don't tell everyone I was a bull rider. It just doesn't seem to come up all that often. When I do, they always ask me the same question: "What were you thinking?"

What was I thinking! I'm not sure, but I know that I wanted to experience what it was like to ride a bull. It wasn't a one-time thing. I not only wanted to experience riding a bull, I wanted to excel at the sport. How did I come to such an irrational decision? Did I not understand the dangers associated with bull-riding? The answer is, I did, and I still wanted to make bull-riding a part of my life.

What was I thinking is the first lesson I learned from bull-riding. When I start a new project, I always ask the management team, *What do you want to have happen?* Interestingly, most haven't thought about it much. They don't really know! What do you want to have happen, is one of the most difficult questions that leaders, managers, and individuals need to answer. It's called having a vision.

Most business leaders walk me to a nicely framed, well-worded document hanging on the wall in their lobby and then proceed to read it to me. I find it interesting when the leader of the business hasn't memorized his own vision. What about the employees? Do they even know it's there and what it means? Creating a compelling, implementable vision is the first objective.

Decisions

I have spent a great deal of time observing and trying to understand the process of thinking—how we make decisions, how we as individuals think. What makes each of us different when it comes to thinking? Why are there so many differences of opinions and how do these opinions affect decision making?

What I discovered is that we think and make decisions in three distinctively different ways or methods:

1. *Common Sense Decisions*

2. *Knowledge-Based Decisions*

3. *Impulse-Based Decisions*

Common Sense Decisions

> Common sense is seeing things as they are
> and doing things as they ought to be.
>
> —Harriet Beecher Stowe
> American abolitionist and author

From childhood, we develop a mental image of how the world around us is or should be. We identify how we interact with it and what is acceptable and unacceptable. With time, these ideals and values become our way of life; they become our common sense. Common sense is taking an umbrella if the forecast calls for rain, taking water along on a hike, and looking both ways when crossing a street.

These are common sense decisions we make every day. We don't really think about our gift of common sense. We develop it naturally over time.

Knowledge-Based Decisions

When it comes to gaining knowledge, we learn in a variety of ways.

> There are three types of men—the one that learns from reading—the few that learn from observation—and the rest of us who have to pee on the electric fence for ourselves.
>
> —Will Rogers

Most of us have attended or will attend school sometime our lives. We will study a variety of subjects while becoming educated and will choose to gain deeper knowledge on a few of them. Add to that knowledge our life experiences, and this in total becomes our education, our knowledge of the world around us.

From this knowledge, we make decisions every day. The doctor makes decisions that save lives. The lawyer makes decisions based on his or her knowledge of the law. Each of us makes decisions based on the education we've received and the knowledge we develop. We make decisions that are founded in consistent facts that have been proven to be true.

Impulse-Based Decisions

The third way we make decisions is by impulse. If someone is impulsive, it means they act on instinct without thinking decisions through. Letting your 16-year-old borrow the car for the first time may be an impulsive decision you'll regret later!

You know you are about to experience an impulse decision when you hear someone say something like "Here, hold my beer and watch this!" (I recommend you get this on video—it is going to be worth seeing again later. It might also come in handy when you are trying to explain to the doctor what actually happened.)

We make impulsive decisions every day. Impulsive decision-making is seen as acting on a whim or being impulsive. This type of decision-making, most of the time anyway, is considered a negative personality trait and one we are encouraged to suppress.

But the truth is our brains are developed to include all three types of decision making. All three are important and necessary, and we should develop the ability to use all three methods. Our thinking, reasoning, and decision-making are what make us unique and human.

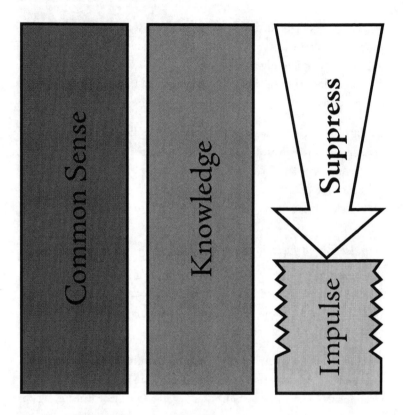

Balanced-Thinking Decisions

Balanced-thinking is the ability to leverage all three types or modes of thinking when making decisions. Mastering this aptitude is extremely effective when you are developing a vision for yourself or an organization or when identifying next-level opportunities.

Picture a group of pizza-chain executives sitting in a boardroom, developing their marketing strategy, when one of them asks the all-important question: "What do we want to have happen?" Their overwhelming response: "To be the most successful pizza company ever." (Impulse)

How would we accomplish that? "By giving our customers better pizza and service than anyone else." (Knowledge)

How could we measure that superior service? "Deliver pizza in 30 minutes or it's free!" (Common Sense)

Sounds impulsive—too bold to work! Right?

Domino's Pizza had a wild impulse: To promise customers "Pizza delivered in 30 minutes or it's free." Had the execs pushed down their impulse and led with knowledge and common sense first, they might have come up with "Hot pizza delivered fresh to your door."

Instead, Domino's Pizza redefined the pizza industry with the bolder, balanced-thinking claim, giving them the potential for market leadership, which they achieved.

Consider where you are leading your organization. Is it market-changing or are you playing it safe? Organizations that lead with balanced-thinking visions have the potential to change the world. What is your balanced-thinking answer to the toughest tough question, *What do you want to have happen?*

As I consider what went through my mind on the day I made the decision to get on my first bull, the logical answer would be it must have been an *impulse* decision. A *step aside and watch this* moment. But that wasn't the case. I wanted to experience the thrill of bull-riding, and to my way of thinking, it was well worth the risk.

My impulse answer to the question what do you want to have happen? was I want to ride a bull and win the event! It wasn't just to stare death in the face and survive; I wanted to be a bull rider, for hell's sake. (Impulse) The knowledge and common sense came later as I learned what it would take to become a winning bull rider.

I would need to know what was necessary and where to get my own gear. (Knowledge) I joined the South Fremont High School Rodeo Team. Finally, I would need to learn how to stay on a bucking bull for 8 long seconds. Practice! (Common Sense)

Another way to more fully understand balanced-thinking is to examine the type of activities that might appear on your bucket list.

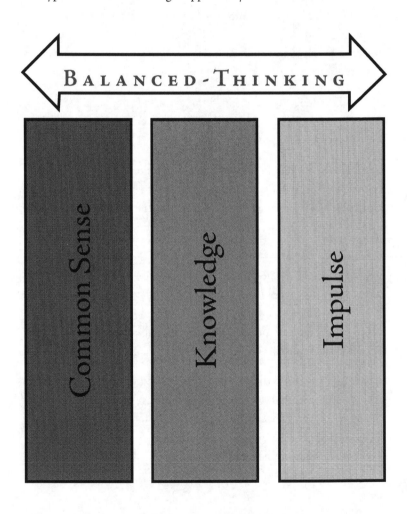

Usually, this list is made up of things that may be considered to be bold or a bit dangerous, like sky diving, mountain climbing, or driving a Formula One racecar. Maybe it is to visit the South American ruins of Machu Picchu or to take a train ride across the Rocky Mountains. Maybe it is to see the great pyramids of Egypt.

Regardless of your interests, I hope you have a bucket list, and I hope it has some very exciting things on it. Bull-riding was one of my bucket list items before I knew what a bucket list was. The question is, how do these items get on your bucket list in the first place?

Proactive vs. Reactive

Learning to become a balanced thinker is not as easy as it sounds. Starting from a blank sheet can be intimidating and requires proactive thinking, something most of us don't practice very often. We are much better at reactive thinking. We are being programmed every day by our portable devices to react—react to situations, react to choices, and react to resolve conflicts.

When I ask what do you want to have happen, which is the toughest of questions, you are left to proactively develop your own response. I've laid it out with nothing for you to react to—no options to choose from.

Proactive thinking is a very different skillset than reactive thinking. If I would have given you some potential answers or choices such as 1) go shopping, 2) grab some lunch, or 3) go for a bike ride, you would have been able to respond quickly and without much consideration. We are all good at responsive or reactive thinking.

Starting with a blank page is much more difficult. We see this play out every time we ask our partner where he or she wants to go for dinner. The answer is practically always the same: "Oh, I don't care." And then the responding question comes: "Where do you want to go?" To which you respond with "Chinese sounds good." And they predictably respond with something like "No, we had that last time." And so it goes. Giving a response to a stated set of choices is far easier than conjuring up a proactive answer.

Consider for a moment our three methods of thinking, common sense, knowledge, and impulse. Ask yourself the question again: *What do you want to have happen?* Pay close attention as your mind goes first to impulse thinking for an answer. These impulse answers are usually quite grand in nature, like, *I want to change the world! I want to find a cure for cancer! I want to invent the next great Internet app!*

Our minds then quickly apply the other two thinking methods of knowledge and common sense. We unconsciously question, rethink, and suppress our impulse answer, settling on a much less aggressive response like *I want to get a better job. I want to lose ten pounds. I want to buy a new computer.*

I call this non-balanced-thinking pattern *Conform to the Norm.* We don't want to stand out. We want to be seen as normal, like everyone else. We don't embrace our impulse response because, heaven forbid, we may be seen as being impulsive.

Some of us have the natural ability to leverage the three methods of thinking to achieve balanced-thinking. Those who have this natural ability are called *visionaries.* They paint a picture for the rest of us to follow. They envision new products, invent countless unique items, and solve the mysteries of the universe. They possess the ability to suppress their common-sense, and knowledge-thinking methods just long enough to consider *what if, why not, and how would I.*

Developing this balanced-thinking approach opens the door to other, proactive possibilities. Possibilities we otherwise wouldn't have considered.

On the day when I decided to become a bull rider, I applied balanced-thinking. Surely common sense should have won the day, but it didn't. From one balanced-thinking decision, I have an indelible memory that changed my life.

Our ability to visualize is incredibly important for those leadership opportunities. We are all pressed to be leaders. We are brothers and sisters, moms and dads, husbands and wives, soccer coaches, cheerleaders, school board members, and students. The leadership opportunity list is endless, and it includes all of us. We can be significantly more effective in these roles if we develop and hone our ability to create balanced-thinking visions.

Practice this balanced-thinking method. If you will, two things will happen. First, you may well reprogram your brain's thinking patterns as you challenge yourself to become a proactive vs. a reactive thinker.

Second, you will experience the feeling of control. You will feel the excitement of having a personal vision. You will see the milestones needed to achieve success, even if just for one day. This proactive, balanced-thinking approach will change everything.

Share your vision with someone else, and see if they too are not caught up in the excitement. They will check in on you to see how you are doing. We are all naturally attracted to a compelling, common vision.

Team Player Choice

While working on a project with the Newcomb Consulting Group, I was introduced to the Team-Player-Choice model. This model provides a clear explanation as to why vision is so important when working with groups, organizations, or teams.

The model has four quadrants, and the headings are Fully In, Situational, Non and Pretender.

"Fully In" are those times when we are fully behind the vision and supporting the cause. You have our undivided attention!

"Situational" means that, depending on the situation, I will choose to engage (or not). I want the cause to be directed in a certain way or with certain individuals.

"Non" is simply that. I choose not to show up!

"Pretender" is the most dangerous box. When you occupy the pretender box, you act as if you are "Fully In," but in fact you are not. Others may

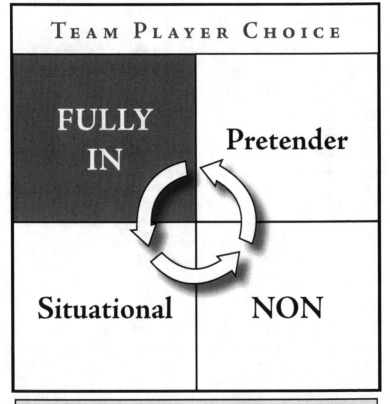

TEAM PLAYER CHOICE

FULLY IN

Pretender

Situational

NON

—Newcomb Consulting Group

be counting on you because you expressed your support, but in reality you elected not to truly become engaged.

In any given initiative or situation, we occupy one of these four quadrants. Depending on our understanding of what is being presented, we position ourselves in terms of our engagement or willingness to participate. We can and do move from quadrant to quadrant throughout the process.

Initially, maybe we want to be on the team, "Fully In"; but as time goes by, we lose interest. Without a compelling vision and goal, we become distracted or disillusioned. We choose to step out. We become "Situational" or choose the "NON" box, no longer wanting to be a member of the team. Even worse, we become a *pretender*, acting as if we are engaged when in reality we never intend to do the work.

Can you see the impact this repositioning dynamic can have on the progress of an initiative? Having to identify which quadrant everyone's in and having to re-engage individuals as they choose to move between the quadrants, you're trying to find what caused their thinking and engagement to shift. This shifting around can zap the energy out of a team and cause most initiatives to slow down or stop completely.

When initiatives start with a compelling vision, we as team members choose the "Fully In" box. The vision serves as a guidepost to keep the team on track. There aren't quadrant shifts when the vision is clear. Milestones are clearly identified and measured. Accountability is supported by the team as progress is made toward the goal.

Financial Visions

If you own the company or you are a "C"- level executive, a CEO or CFO for example, your vision usually includes a financial declaration like "We want to hit $150 million in sales revenues within five years."

This is a valid, balanced-thinking goal. However, if you are a lower-level employee, it doesn't have much significance. Maybe it would if you're a sales professional and get a bonus based on hitting the company's revenue targets. If not, you get paid the same amount every two weeks regardless of the company revenues. So, the vision of 150 in 5 won't inspire everyone in the organization.

Explore how the company would be different after hitting the 150 in 5 financial milestone as the foundation and build your balanced-thinking vision from that.

When you want to energize the entire organization, have everyone be "Fully In", make the goal something everyone can relate to, contribute to, and share in.

By practicing balanced-thinking, I was able to create a compelling vision and experience the thrill of bull-riding.

Where will your balanced-thinking vision take you?
Don't wait to find out.

GETTING ON THE BULL
How To Create a Compelling Vision

Now that you understand what a balanced-thinking vision is, it's time to create a compelling vision of your own.

It's time to get on the bull!

> *When the creative impulse sweeps over you, grab it. You grab it, honor it, and use it, because momentum is a rare gift.*
>
> —Justina Chen, author and speaker

Experience has taught me that when creating a vision, the bigger the better. I'm not talking about the number of words it takes to communicate the vision, but rather how far you or your organization needs to stretch to achieve it. The balanced-thinking approach will help you create a vision—a vision that will spur excitement about your future.

If it is time to change things up a bit, start with a compelling vision. One that excites you and engages others. One where everyone is "Fully In."

Creating a compelling vision that will inspire you and others requires some effort on your part. If you really want to achieve something great, ask yourself, what do I want, is it worth the personal effort, and am I willing to hold myself and others accountable?

As I stated earlier, a compelling vision has three parts; the impulse vision statement itself, *what do you want to have happen*; the knowledge statement, *how you are going to achieve the vision*; and the common-sense statement, *how you are going to measure progress*.

Have you ever started down the path to a goal? You're determined to see it through when somewhere along the way the vision simply disappeared.

Something changed, and your goal was no longer relevant. What happened? Why were you not successful?

My guess is you fell off the path for one of these three reasons:

You didn't

1. *Clearly identify the goal or objective,*

2. *Know what's required to achieve it,*

3. *Create KPIs (Key Performance Indicators) for personal or organizational accountability.*

These three steps provide the path for not only identifying, but achieving a compelling vision. Work your way through each step and develop your balanced-thinking vision.

Question: *What do you want to have happen?*

> *Begin with the end in mind.*
>
> —Stephen Covey

Identify the Goal

"All things are created twice. We create them first in our minds, and then we work to bring them into physical existence. By taking control of our own first creation, we can write or rewrite our own scripts, thus taking some control and responsibility for the outcome."

Don't limit your initial vision. Give yourself time to experience what your impulse-thinking is challenging you to consider. Don't jump to knowledge-thinking (strategy) and common-sense (measurement) too quickly. Hold on to your impulse, and think BIG. Don't hold back. Learn to embrace impulse-thinking.

Keep your desired outcome direct, simple, and concise. Long, rambling vision statements show you haven't done the difficult work of identifying what is really important. This will take time, so don't rush it.

Today, our communication style is short and to the point. Think text messages. When it comes to your vision, I find it is better to just say it like it is.

I want my company to be great, I'm going to start my own business, I'm going to get my degree, or maybe I want to be a bull rider!

I'm sure if you think for a minute, you can name individuals who are, for one reason or another, successful. Consider their path. What did they do to create success? It most likely started with a compelling vision.

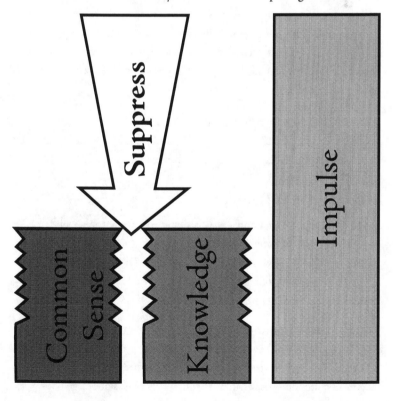

Can you name a few companies that have embraced their impulse-thinking and created amazing visions? I'm sure you can.

Consider UBER, the most successful startup in history. UBER'S vision was to leverage the global issue of finding people rides, using other people's cars, putting them at the right place at the right time, and connecting them to each other via the Internet. **What a compelling vision!**

A personal favorite is BIG ASS FANS, a Midwest manufacturer of large warehouse fans. I like how they just say it like it is. These companies were born just this way. Simply answering the question, What do you want to have happen?

Ask yourself the questions at the end of this paragraph. Keep knowledge and common sense at bay. Really listen to your thoughts and write down the answer. Think to yourself, *if I could only do one thing every day for the rest of my life, what would that be? What is the one thing I was put on this earth to do?*

What is your impulse-thinking answer? _____

_____

_____

Know What is Required

Apply the method of knowledge-thinking to your impulse answer. Be careful not to change your impulse answer, but rather to refine it to better reflect your current condition and to ensure it is personally relevant. Keep in mind, this vision will change your life. If you embrace your impulse, you will never be the same again.

Once you have decided on your impulse answer, identify what will be required to achieve the goal. Write down everything you can think of. Don't let this activity change your impulse answer. Remember, knowledge and common sense tend to encourage us to lessen our goals.

After you have identified as many activities as possible, it's time to identify the three most critical to achieving the goal. Start by combining and crossing out activities that are one-time tasks, like getting a gym membership, taking a class, or identifying a good location for your new venture.

Identify the activities that can be considered differentiators. What three critical activities, when accomplished, set you apart from the crowd and drive you toward the goal?

These few critical activities are the ones you will need to do multiple times or practice to perfection. These are the tasks that, if not identified early, will over time wear you down. It's good to know what you are getting yourself into before you start, insuring you are ready for the journey—to make sure you are all in.

My decision to become a bull-rider was solidified in my mind long before I slid down onto my first bull. I had prepared myself both mentally and physically. It was the moment I had been waiting for, and I was ready for the ride.

Although I quickly found out how unprepared I was, my desire to ride for the coveted eight seconds was only cemented deeper into my resolve.

Create KPIs

As your developing vision becomes clearer, you'll next want to identify how long the initiative might take. When will you achieve the goal? Be realistic but aggressive. Remember this is a balanced-thinking vision. You are going to focus all your efforts on achieving it. Dragging it out will only make it harder and less likely to be achieved.

Like any good strategy, if you want to succeed, milestones must be set along the way. Use knowledge-thinking to identify the critical milestones required for achieving the goal.

If your vision is for your company, identify the impact your vision will have on the financials, departments, business processes, customers, and employees. Are there milestones relating to each of these that need to be identified?

Keep the number of KPIs to 5 or less. By setting a limit, you will focus on those critical indicators that really matter. Focusing on them daily will insure traction and success.

If your vision is for your company, this is the point where you want to include the organization in developing your KPIs. It is very important to involve the organization in the vision-development process, making it their vision as well as yours.

Let's consider an example from one of my past clients: Their impulse statement was "I want my company to be great." (Impulse Statement) Consider the value, impact, and importance this impulse vision statement would have on the organization.

We next applied knowledge-thinking to identify the critical requirements needed to reach the goal. Remember, the list should be concise to provide focus.

"The Vision for our Company is to be Great—through Engineering Excellence, World Class Manufacturing, and Proud Customers and Employees." (Knowledge Statement)

Finally, it was time to share their vision with the company to add the finishing touches, completing their balanced-thinking vision statement. The organization assisted by focusing on how the vision would be measured. We included statements in the vision that would drive them forward; milestones and measurements helped to accomplish that.

It is extremely important to have measurable items in your vision statement. It shows you are serious and have defined the results you want to achieve. Include statements that not only have meaning to your employees, but to your customers as well. The vision should include statements that can be measured so progress toward the goal is clear and evident.

To complete this balanced-thinking example, we included common-sense measurables:

The Vision for our Company is to be Great through

1. *Engineering Excellence*
   We Don't Miss Dates

2. *World Class Manufacturing*
   Zero Defects at Pre-Customer Runoff

3. *Proud Employees and Customers*
   We are the Company of Choice

Each statement in this vision is straight-forward, concise, and measurable. This vision creates excitement, focus, and can absolutely be realized. This is a Balanced-Thinking Vision.

CREATE A COMPELLING VISION
Embrace Balanced-thinking!
+ *Identify Your Goal*
+ *Know what is Required*
+ *Create KPI's*

CONCLUSION

Having a long, well written, vision statement isn't as effective as having one that is concise, one that can be easily memorized, one that can be aligned with, and one that can be measured. Don't try to make it flowery. Just state it as it is!

Insure the vision is relevant to your current situation. Does it have value, and will it make a difference in the lives of your employees and your customers? To be successful, it has to matter.

Don't sign up for a vision you're not passionate about achieving. Give it your undivided attention, making sure others see, hear, feel, and think you are completely committed to achieving the goal. Just stating it isn't enough, even if it's a great vision.

From personal experience as a trainer, I learned that you must deliver your material with a level of enthusiasm that is two levels above your audience. That's right, two levels of enthusiasm *above* where you want the audience to be! They will unconsciously position themselves two levels of enthusiasm below where you are.

Have you ever listened to a speaker with a low enthusiasm level? Regardless of the topic, it probably felt tired and boring, and your attention faded away.

When speakers are excited and energized about their topic, regardless of what the topic is, we are captivated and drawn into their world. TED Talks have mastered this phenomenon of drawing you into a topic.

If you want your vision to become a reality, GET EXCITED!

Maybe your company already has a vision statement. For practice, let's examine a random company's vision statement.

"Our VISION, quite simply, is to be: The World's Premier Food Company Offering Nutritious, Superior Tasting Foods to People Everywhere; being the premier food company does not mean being the biggest, but it does mean being the best in terms of consumer value, customer service, employee talent, and consistent and predictable growth."

This vision, while descriptive, does not create much excitement. Can you see common sense and knowledge taking over?

There are no claims of greatness, no leader statement, no claim of being a pace-setter. It will be difficult for an employee to memorize, difficult to align themselves, with and provides no way to measure how their daily activities drive the company toward success.

What it does say is they are not striving to be the biggest. And their definition of *the best* isn't measured against anyone or anything. In other words, it states that they want to be the same as every other food company while staying below the radar.

Unfortunately, this is often what I find when working with troubled companies. Is it any wonder they are struggling?

Let's see if we can apply our balanced-thinking approach and rework the vision. First, identify the words that create excitement. Words like *world's or global, premier, value, service, and growth*. Then apply balanced-thinking by using those words to create excitement. Finally, let's add some measurables for relevancy.

Our New Vision
Be the Global Standard of Premier Nutrition

Our Three-Fold Mission is to deliver
Value (The best product, period, or your money back);
Service (Delivered to anywhere in the world);
Growth (By empowered, accountable employees).

Without too much effort, and by simply making a few adjustments, we completely changed the energy of the vision. It is now bold, it is now measurable, and it now provides the required focus to get people excited about the goal of becoming a Premier Food Company.

Making the decision to ride bulls takes balanced-thinking. Take your company's vision, give it a balanced-thinking rewrite, and get your organization excited about their future.

CREATE A COMPELLING VISION
The first lesson of Boardroom Bullrider!

BOARDROOM
BULLRIDER

LESSON 2

INTIMIDATION
ELIMINATE YOUR INTIMIDATORS

Possesses strong, dedicated, and focused leadership qualities positioning oneself clearly in front of the organization reinforcing the vision and modeling the way."

Pre-Assessment:
Eliminate Your Intimidators

❐ The leadership/management team is dedicated to the financial targets.

❐ The leadership/management team is competent to achieve identified objectives.

❐ The leadership/management team is committed to their own personal objectives.

❐ The leadership/management team develops strong internal and external relationships.

❐ The leadership/management team is accountable for keeping their agreements.

❐ The leadership/management team communicates clearly, consistently, and respectfully.

The Strength: _____

The Weakness: _____

The Opportunity: _____

The Threat: _____

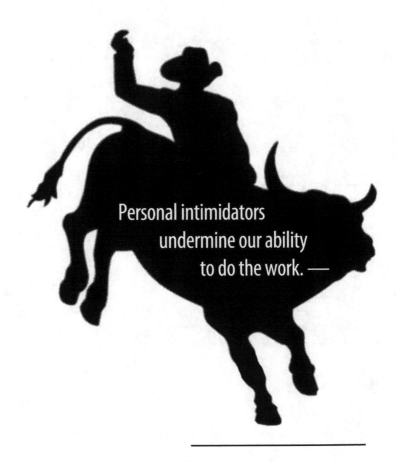

Personal intimidators
undermine our ability
to do the work. ——

During my life as a bull rider, there were many times I was intimidated. It's part of the sport. Watching the rider one bull ahead of you get slammed hard on his back in the dirt, crawl out of the arena, and sit head-down in the corner, trying to recover, is a bit intimidating. But now it's your turn. You have to push the scene out of your head and nod for the gate.

Looking down from the back of the chute at the bull you are getting ready to ride is extremely intimidating, especially when the bull has large horns. Your mind can conjure up all kinds of potentially bad things that might happen to you.

A mentally tough bull rider pushes through the uncertainty, the what-ifs, and you-mights. Otherwise, he would never get on a bull. It's all about the love of the sport and winning the coveted buckle.

To ride a bull, you are required to hold on with only one hand. The other hand can never touch the bull. The bull rope is a rather thin, braided rope with a handhold woven into it.

You carefully slide down onto the bull by relaxing your legs and lowering your body, using only your arms, much like a gymnast on the parallel bars. You shove your riding hand into the braided rope and adjust it to find the best grip possible. The rope is pulled tight, and your hand is pinned against the bull's back.

The final step is to take your wrap. The tail of the rope goes around your wrist and back into your open hand. Closing your hand, you lock the grip by pushing your thumb over your fingers. When you nod your head and the gate blows open, you are quite literally tied to the back of the bull.

That's where I learned about beating intimidation. Being tied to a 2000-pound, four-legged mass of muscle with horns that's looking to stomp me into the dirt and then being turned loose into the arena—now that's intimidation.

Intimidation

Back in 1976, while riding in the "Days of 47" Rodeo in St. Anthony, Idaho, I drew a bull named "Sanchez." Sanchez was a big, strong bull with the reputation of being extremely mean. He had large horns that had the ends cut off, leaving about 6 inches of horn as big around as a baseball bat. Get hit by one of those, and it would be *lights out*!

He would throw the rider off and quickly return to find him, then focus on getting to the bucked-off cowboy before he could make it to the fence. Many times, Sanchez went right through the clowns to get to the rider. He would chase the lucky bull riders over the fence and out of the arena. The unlucky ones found themselves getting ploughed into the dirt by Sanchez's baseball-bat horns. No matter what the clowns did to distract Sanchez, it simply didn't work.

Earlier that year, a bull rider hung up on Sanchez. In other words, the cowboy's hand didn't come out of the rope when he fell off. This is a very bad situation to find oneself in. You try to stay on your feet, running alongside the bull, while getting stepped on and being flung around like a rag doll.

That night, Sanchez hit the rider in the head with the blunt end of his horn and knocked the cowboy unconscious. His limp body was dragged alongside, his legs and feet getting stepped on as Sanchez continued to buck.

The clowns tried frantically to get his hand loose. One clown ran along the opposite side, jumping for the tail of the rope to free the rider's hand while trying to avoid the bull's hooves.

Another clown ran in front of Sanchez grabbing at his horns to get him to turn and slow down. The third clown tried to carry the cowboy along by putting his hands under his arm-pits in an attempt to keep him upright and out from under the bull. The crowd was hushed. Most covered their mouths, and some covered their eyes, hoping it would soon be over.

Finally, after several tenuous minutes where time stood still, the gutsy clowns were able to free the rider's hand. A cowboy on horseback roped Sanchez and pulled him into the holding pens. There is always an ambulance waiting outside the arena just in case. That night, the bull rider was carefully carried out of the arena on a stretcher and taken to a nearby hospital. He would be okay, but was out of action for a few weeks.

The memory of that night and the rider being stomped on by Sanchez was stuck in my head. I needed to focus on the job at hand. I tried drawing my attention away by imagining the moves Sanchez would make and how I would counteract them. I was focused on making the 8 seconds.

My turn at Sanchez finally came, and I carefully slid down on him. His back felt flatter than other bulls I had been on. It felt solid like sitting on a slab of concrete. He was one of those bulls that would stand calmly in the chute, but you knew he was going to explode as soon the gate was opened.

As I worked getting ready, my mind was focused on that first jump. I wanted to make sure not to get behind. The other bull riders hovered over me, helping to get everything ready. They knew Sanchez as well as I did, and we all knew what he was capable of. I needed everything to go right if I was to have a chance. My buddies were slapping me on the back, telling me to "Cowboy Up" on this one.

I knew exactly how to tie my hand in as I had been on a number of bulls by now. The rope was pulled tight, and I took a little extra time taking my wrap. I wanted it to be just right. I had seen what would happen if I was to get hung-up.

Gritting my teeth, I slid up onto my rope. This riding position of having my hand under my crotch had become comfortable to me. I had taught my body how to relax under the pressure and to calm my mind. Tonight wasn't the same. This ride was different. This ride was serious. I had never been on the back of a bull this dangerous.

That night on the back of Sanchez, intimidation hit me like a freight train and right at the point when the chute boss was expecting me to nod my head. I wasn't able to nod. I sat there like a statue, frozen on the back of this bull. I actually considered holding onto the chute gate as it swung open using it to get off. I asked myself, was this really worth the risk?

Right then and there, sitting on the back of Sanchez, one of the rankest bulls I knew, I learned how to beat intimidation. I had to act. That was the counter-move I needed to push through my fear.

I took another deep breath. The grandstand was as quiet as a church. Everyone was watching me now, waiting for me to go. I looked up into the faces of the cowboys standing beside me for some last-minute encouragement. Then, reaching down deep inside myself, I found the courage to nod my head. In that very instant, the chute latch cracked like the sound of a gun, and the big gate swung open. It was game on!

In a split second, Sanchez went from standing calmly in the chute to exploding into the arena. Everyone was yelling. I threw my body forward making it past the first jump. My head was down, looking at his shoulders. Out of the corner of my eye, I saw Sanchez swing his head around into a right-hand spin. I forced my focus back onto his shoulders. My experience and preparation were paying off. My intimidation had turned into determination.

8 Seconds is a Really Long Time

I was in the zone. Time had slipped into slow motion. Sanchez continued to the right. His horns were now mere inches away from my leg as he swung his head around. I could see my next counter-move coming; this meant I was taking the power away from the bull. It felt as though I was predicting his every move.

This powerful bull would be mine. I was matching Sanchez jump for jump. That's when it happened—in all the excitement I thought to myself, *Where is that 8-second buzzer? Have I missed it?*

In that instant, I lost my focus. Somehow Sanchez knew it and cranked it back hard to the left, out of the spin. I was suddenly thrown to the arena floor. As I was hit the ground, I heard the buzzer go off in the judge's booth. 7.2 seconds!

I felt my shoulder hit the dirt first followed by the rest of my body. I was stunned and woozy from the impact of hitting the ground. You know that feeling you get when you bump your head really hard? It's nothing like that. It's more like getting hit in the head with a baseball bat, then attempting to run away as fast as you can. There is no sitting and rubbing your head until your eyes stop watering and the ringing in your ears quit. You have to get the heck out of there!

I struggled to get to my feet. It was a bit difficult to stand up and steady myself. I knew Sanchez would be looking for me, which added to my dazed confusion. I looked up and saw Sanchez coming at me from across the arena. Even worse, I didn't see any clowns!

As I struggled to run, my feet sank into the loose dirt, causing me to fall down again. My legs were shaky from the impact, and it felt like I had rocks in my pockets. Reaching the chutes, I lunged at the top rail. Sanchez brushed my legs as I pulled myself over the top of the fence.

Sanchez won that night; however, I learned to overcome my fears because I had turned my intimidation into determination. I learned to fight through one of the most intimidating moments I would ever have as a bull rider to experience the ride of my life.

That night I guess we both won!

Eliminate Your Intimidators

Great leaders quoted in business books all have one thing in common, a strong desire to act. They are viewed as great because they were willing to push through intimidation and make the tough decisions.

Ted Turner saw the possibility of 24-hour news before anyone else did. All the ingredients were there. Despite the skeptics' advice, Turner made a tough decision, stepped into the arena, connected the dots, and created CNN.

As we observe other great leaders, it's obvious they don't know the outcome or the full impact of their decisions at the time they are made. What makes them great leaders is their willingness to push forward through intimidation by doing the most-right thing at the time.

We have all experienced intimidation. Remember the first time you climbed the ladder of the high dive? It wasn't that tall when looking at it from the deck. Once you were at the edge of the board looking down into the water, your perspective changed. You now seem so far above the water.

I'll bet you turned around to see if climbing back down the ladder was an option. But the next diver was already there. Isn't that about how it happened?

The only way to get past intimidation was to jump. Take a step forward and experience the rush. Once you jump, you are committed, not intimidated. You overcome or eliminate your intimidator and move on. Apply this same strategy to making tough decisions.

When faced with a tough decision, there are usually a variety of possible solutions. Most difficult problems cannot be solved with one simple decision or action. They require multiple steps or actions to be taken.

Do The Most-Right Thing Now

Do the most-right thing now is about taking that first step, taking action, not waiting for the chance to solve the entire problem in one giant leap. By the way, that rarely happens.

Great leaders are always moving toward the goal. Step by step, they remain focused on achieving success by doing the most-right thing at the time and not getting distracted by trivial, insignificant tasks. They don't let intimidation get in the way.

> *You can always count on Americans to do the right thing—after they've tried everything else.*
>
> —Winston Churchill

He may have been right. The question is this: Are you doing the "most-right" thing first, or are you doing what is most convenient?

Are you intimidated by the most-right thing so you choose the safer answer? Great leaders make decisions at the time the decision needs to be made—when the situation is critical, when the decision will have the greatest impact.

A lot of things today intimidate us into complacency: Fear of the unknown. Not wanting to hear bad news. Knowing what will be expected once you start.

I find one of the biggest intimidators to decision making is information. The Internet Age provides us with unlimited data. You can Google and get information on any topic. We are, or at least should be, the smartest generation that has ever lived on the earth.

This vast amount of information can be intimidating at times, especially when a tough decision is at hand. I call it *data-overload*. There is so much information available to us that we can, in most cases, prove any decision to be the correct one. This gets to be confusing, overwhelming, and intimidating when you are required to make that all-important decision that affects employees, customers, vendors, and key stakeholders. How do you choose when any decision can be proven to be the right one?

I have observed companies that simply can't make a decision. They hold endless meetings to discuss possible solutions, only to adjourn to evaluate the situation further. Or they push the decision out to a future date, relieving them of having to deal with it now.

As I learned on the back of Sanchez that night long ago, the only way to eliminate your intimidators is to act.

ACT—Action Changes Things

We make decisions every day. Some are simple, easy to decide, and have little impact—what to eat for lunch or which way to drive home after work.

When it comes to making tough decisions—should I go back to college? should I change jobs? should we spend millions on a new marketing campaign?—you must push through intimidation, decide on a course, and act. You can't drive a parked car. Once you have it moving, you have unlimited options. Don't be intimidated. It may take a number of smaller decisions and adjustments to achieve the final goal.

Step 1: Take a step forward. *Do the most-right thing now.*

You make the decision, and the required action is taken, everything changes. The field of view is different. You gain new information. You get to see, in real time, the result of your initial decision.

At times we are intimidated with the fact that we might make the wrong decision. Experience has taught me that making a wrong decision is better than no decision at all.

> *Whenever you see a successful business,*
> *someone once made a courageous decision.*
>
> —Peter F. Drucker,
> founder of modern management

You will never know the outcome of your decision if you don't make one. Choose the *most-right* action to take and learn from the outcome.

Step 2: Observe. *Observe the results of our decision.*

What changed? What stayed the same? Are we any closer to our intended result? You are now in a position to evaluate the impact of the initial decision. Don't be too quick to judge the correctness of the action you've taken. Give the dust time to settle. Great leaders always talk about their mistakes. Why? Those mistakes usually lead to an even greater outcome because of the knowledge gained.

Keep the overall objective in mind. If you are moving closer to the objective, reinforce the path you have chosen. If you are moving away from the objective, understand the factors causing you to distance yourself. These factors are critical to the next decision you will need to make for a course correction. Do not dwell too long on the positive or the negative impact made.

Step 3: Adjust. *Once you have observed the impact, make the necessary adjustments to course-correct.*

Stay focused on the intended course. I consider any decision a good decision as long as adjustments are made to maintain direction. These adjustments need to be focused on the critical issues that are causing you to drift away.

I've observed companies that, when a decision wasn't producing the intended results, executed a complete redesign. Everything was reevaluated to create a new path. This is where the term "deal-of-the-day" comes from. The decision makers are labeled and viewed by others as always changing their minds. This can cripple organizational momentum because employees quickly lose trust in management.

Step 4: Consider. *Consider you next move.*

If your previous decision is delivering the intended outcome, your next-step decision will involve reinforcing the direction, identifying short-term wins, and celebrating the success.

If the decision is not delivering the intended result, make the necessary adjustments. The next-step decision needed will include reinforcing those critical adjustments, evaluating their effectiveness, and creating momentum.

Trust = Character and Competence

Making decisions or, in this case, not making them isn't the only issue you face when you are intimidated. When you are intimidated, you become, as the word suggests, timid. Being timid isn't considered a strong leadership quality. When you move past your intimidators, you are no longer timid and can act with confidence, thus building the trust others have in your ability to deliver.

Stephen Covey Jr. developed the example on page 49 of how using "character" and "competence" builds trust when enlisting others. I have modified it to illustrate what happens when we are timid in character or in competence. The result is the same. We lose trust and become less effective as a leader

The figure on page 49, (left side, inward focused) reflects an individual having strong character and weak competence. Your intentions are clear and strengthened by your integrity. This individual works well with others; maybe the phrase "is liked by all" is used when describing the person. However, being weak in competence, he or she may struggle to get results.

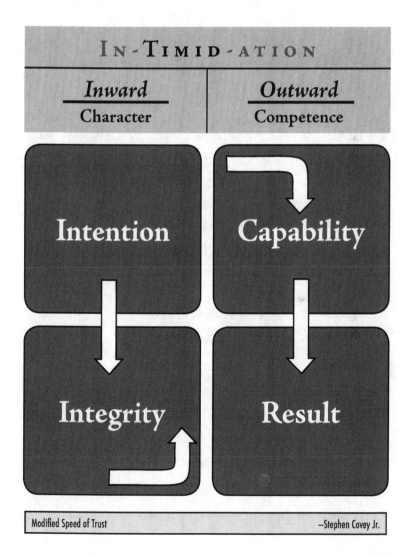

IN-TIMID-ATION

| Inward | Outward |
| Character | Competence |

Intention

Capability

Integrity

Result

Modified Speed of Trust —Stephen Covey Jr.

Inward intimidators may include individuals exhibiting the fear of failure or the fear of making a poor decision. Maybe they're intimidated when singled out or asked to present in front of a group. You are a team player but not a team leader.

On the other hand, individuals who are strong in competence and weak in character, (right side, outward focused) have the capability to get results but may leave a path of destruction in their wake. People describe them as "getting results."

Outward intimidators may have trouble working on teams. You're frustrated having to work cross-functionally, bringing the team along when you're focused on getting to the results. You enjoy presenting your ideas and training others while expressing your capabilities.

Work on both your inward and outward intimidators to balance the scale. When you have character *and* competence, you truly become a leader.

Eliminate your intimidators by focusing on inward intimidators—*Character*, and outward intimidators—*Competence*.

> ### Step into the arena,
> ### eliminate your intimidators,
> ### and take action!

GETTING ON THE BULL
How To Eliminate Your Intimidators

Intimidation isn't always caused by external factors like I experienced when bull-riding. Intimidation can be caused by internal factors as well, those demons from within. Sometimes we need to get square with ourselves and identify what is holding us back.

If you are the leader of your organization, your actions will set the stage and create the pace of change, ultimately determining the outcome. There is an ancient phrase that goes something like this: "The fish stinks from the head down."

As the phrase suggests, your organization will be a reflection of its leader. When the business is doing everything well, everyone is a winner. When everything with the business is going terribly wrong, everyone blames the leader.

If you want to create positive change and build a truly remarkable organization, it starts with you. You must be "Fully In" if you want others to be.

Let's examine the aptitudes of Eliminate Your Intimidators. These aptitudes are designed to beat intimidation and to teach you how to create personal and organizational momentum.

These aptitudes can be focused inward on you personally as an individual, as well as focused outward on your team or organization.

Align your words and actions. *Ensure that your actions reflect your words. Others should see, hear, think, and feel your true intent as your words align with your actions.*

Take personal inventory. *Are you ready? If you're not personally focused on the results, enthusiasm will wane.*

Do the Work. *Be deliberate about what you want, expect, and believe. When you do the work, your path becomes clear.*

These aptitudes help you identify and push through your intimidators. Making timely decisions is critical to the ongoing success of an organization. Without these aptitudes, it's easy to get off track.

Align Your Words and Actions

Once you are clear about your vision and direction, you become capable of communicating your intent to others. Your actions are in alignment with your words.

Example: Have you ever experienced a presentation where the speaker clearly wasn't *bought into* the subject matter? It probably came across as superficial, shallow, and insincere.

Compare that to someone who was *passionate* about their perspective and where the presenter had obviously invested the time to fully comprehend and become enthusiastic about their position.

Intimidation can cause us to be superficial, shallow, and insincere. You must move past those intimidators causing you to question your actions. But first you must identify what your intimidators are. Now that you have a balanced-thinking vision, including your knowledge and common-sense statements, you can start to clearly see those activities that could potentially derail your progress—Intimidators!

Remember, ACT—Action Changes Things.

Let me share with you some examples of intimidators. The example most easily identified with is the desire to lose weight. For most of us, this has been or will be a goal at some point in our lives. We set our goal, identify how we are going to get there, and choose a diet and exercise plan. Success is just around the corner.

Unfortunately, the odds are against us ever achieving this weight-loss goal. Why? What is so hard about diet and exercise? If you have ever been on this path, you know all the intimidators: Pie and ice-cream. Cheesecake. Deep-fried anything. Burgers and fries.

Maybe you are not a morning person and find getting up to exercise extremely difficult when given the choice of the treadmill or the mattress. You come home from work exhausted, and exercise is the last thing on your mind. You grab a snack and head straight for your favorite chair in front of the TV.

If you don't identify your intimidators, all the planning, regardless of the goal, will never produce success. I have met business leaders intimidated with risk taking. They encourage their organizations to "think outside the box" but keep their own shiny wingtips squarely inside.

Aligning your words with your actions requires you to push past your intimidators and create action. Read your balanced-thinking vision and identify the critical requirements that might be a bit intimidating. If you don't address them before embarking on your vision quest, you will most likely not achieve your goal.

Take Personal Inventory

Once you have identified your intimidators, take a personal inventory of yourself. Having dealt with your intimidators, you come across as strong, confident, and committed.

When things get dicey, a common scenario is to push harder. You put on a great game face and tell yourself this will pass—just ignore it and it will all go away. To be an effective leader, you must take control of your personal situation.

Start by pondering and honestly answering these twelve personal inventory questions.

> 1. *Are you content, or are you stressed?*
>
> 2. *Is your life in balance, or are you living from one dramatic episode to another?*
>
> 3. *What is motivating you to move down your current path?*
>
> 4. *Do you live with trust, or do you live in fear of others?*
>
> 5. *Are you holding on to pain from the past, or have you taken time to let go?*
>
> 6. *Is your self-image strong and confident or weak and pessimistic?*
>
> 7. *Do you feel healthy and fit, or do you live as a victim of illness?*
>
> 8. *What is your long-term aim or objective?*
>
> 9. *Is your current direction aligned with your core values?*
>
> 10. *Are you staying authentic and genuine with yourself?*
>
> 11. *Are you leaving your desired legacy?*
>
> 12. *Are you measuring success, or are you reactionary?*

Have you honestly answered these questions? If so, you can now dig beneath the surface of those activities, experiences, and people. Identify the values that underlie them.

Make small, incremental changes to align yourself with your goal. Push through intimidation, and maintain a sense of direction. Focus on the critical activities that propel you toward your goal. Even small adjustments can be extremely empowering.

You will still have times of transition and intimidation, but this gives you the tools to steer yourself out of the rapids and into smoother water.

Taking the action required is one of the essential activities of the control process. If you are intimidated and the results you are getting don't meet your personal standards, your process needs to be altered.

Take the action required to do the work. Don't start any initiative if you are not willing to do the work. I have seen this all too often. Unfortunately, we cheat on ourselves more often than we cheat on others. Don't slip into laziness or procrastination. Get past your intimidators and act.

Do the Work

I often work with individuals who are serious about making a change in their lives or in their businesses. They have a vision of what they want. They have spent the time to map the change process out in their mind. They create excitement by communicating their vision to others.

Unfortunately, this is where it usually ends. When I follow up with them after a few weeks or months, I find the vision has faded. Something distracted them from achieving their goal. These distractions are intimidators. Not everybody falls victim to their intimidators, but it happens more often than not.

Of all the intimidators I have personally experienced or witnessed in others, the biggest intimidator of them all is unwillingness to do the work—giving up as soon as things get difficult. As long as things run smoothly and on track, life is good, and they are all-in. As soon as things get difficult, and they usually do, they stop doing the work.

When this happens, the best way to stay on track is to acknowledge the intimidator and start being accountable to someone else. Tell a friend, colleague, or a trusted advisor what is intimidating you, and ask them to help you push through it. Make an agreement to have them check up on you as often as necessary. Make sure you keep your agreement as this will encourage them to do the same.

Try expressing yourself proactively rather than reactively by using "how to" rather than "if I." Statements like "when I achieve my goal" keep you focused on the process and help you get more accomplished.

When dealing with intimidation, get focused and get excited. Creating enthusiasm is always contagious. When things change, and they always do, make the necessary adjustments and keep doing the work.

ELIMINATE YOUR INTIMIDATORS

Do the Most-Right Thing Now!

- *Align your Words and Actions*
- *Take Personal Inventory*
- *Do the Work*

CONCLUSION

It takes courage to be a bull rider, to push through intimidation and nod your head for the gate. You can't predict every outcome, certainly not when riding a bull. We all have intimidators and for good reason. Intimidators can make us stronger. They provide an opportunity for us to explore our roads less traveled.

Even though you don't know the outcome, you can tip the scale in your favor by leveraging intimidation. The only way to get past intimidation is to push through it. The bull rider tells himself that he is capable of making the ride. Turning intimidation into determination makes his resolve that much stronger.

> *Courage is being scared to death—and saddling up anyway.*
> —John Wayne

We tend to shy away from our intimidators. We treat them as sacred cows. They are what they are, and that is that. If you want to experience greater success and achievement, you have to face up to and **Eliminate Your Intimidators.**

Take a few minutes to identify all your intimidators. Write them down. Arrange them in order of most to least intimidating. Identify the critical intimidators in your life, those that have the most control over you. Identifying them is the first step toward overcoming them.

I hope by now you have a balanced-thinking vision written down from the first lesson. If not, stop here and get one.

Now look at your list of top intimidators. Are any of them standing in the way of your achieving your vision? If so, let's focus on the one or two you will need to overcome.

If your intimidator is public speaking and your vision is to become a CEO, you will need to overcome the intimidation of public speaking. You won't overcome it in a single event, so accept that it will take some time. You must do the work!

What is the most-right thing to do now? Take a public speaking course, start speaking in front of a mirror, or maybe ask to read to a group of kids at a local school. Whatever it is, do the most-right thing now. Don't wait for tomorrow. Get started right away.

To say I was intimidated sitting on the back of Sanchez would be a gross understatement. I was scared to death. I knew there was only one way to get past intimidation: nod my head and experience the ride!

In bull-riding, nodding for the gate is intimidating. Eliminate your intimidators by doing the most-right thing now. ACT and move forward. Do the work!

E L I M I N A T E   Y O U R   I N T I M I D A T O R S
The second lesson of Boardroom Bullrider

BOARDROOM BULLRIDER

LESSON 3

BALANCE
FOCUS ON CRITICAL ISSUES

The ability to execute a plan, idea, model, design, specification, standard, or policy while at the same time identifying and eliminating any or all constraints.

PRE-ASSESSMENT:
FOCUS ON CRITICAL ISSUES

❏ You possess the ability to identify, communicate, and implement a strategic plan.

❏ You have the ability to identify, communicate, and deal with critical issues.

❏ You identify and encourage each other to say no to non-value-adding activities.

❏ You map workflows, simplify activities, and streamline processes.

❏ Management knows what to identify and measure as Key Performance Indicators. (KPIs—No more than five)

❏ You work through any and all impediments, regardless of their nature.

The Strength: _____

The Weakness: _____

The Opportunity: _____

The Threat: _____

If everything is important
then nothing is important —

If there is one lesson every bull rider knows about, it's balance. It's the one thing while being on the back of a bull you pursue but never really achieve. Even so, you are always looking for it.

You quickly learn that you are not going to overpower this animal. Instead, you have to make a series of adjustments or counter-moves if you are going to make the 8-second ride.

When the bull blows out into the arena, he isn't waiting for you to catch up. That bull makes it exceedingly clear; he doesn't want you there. He will try everything from hooking you with his horns to bucking high into the air to get you off his back. You must remain focused on staying relaxed, balanced, and in the center of the bull.

The force of the bull twisting and bucking up and down makes it practically impossible to stay centered. Anticipated counter-moves—putting yourself into a position that, when the bull makes his move, it throws you back into the center—is the only way to ride a bucking bull. Balance, focus, and correctly anticipating his every move will get you to the 8 seconds and, if you score high enough, the wining buckle.

It takes practice to anticipate a bull's next move and in a split second execute a counter-move. You try to predict where the bull will end up as he makes his next jump, trying to position your body in that exact spot when he arrives. If you are wrong, it can be painful.

Get too far back and the force on your arm from the weight of your body will jerk your hand out of the rope and send you flying out the back. Gravity will slam you back to earth in a grunting heap on the arena floor. Out of the corner of your eye, you'll see the bull swing around, lower his head, and come back to finish the job. Your only chance is to run like hell and catch your breath later.

Too far forward and your feet come up. You're lying on his back, Superman style. You will experience the feeling of falling into the abyss, ending up face to face with the bull. Get ready to get hit between the eyes with a sledge hammer. Getting a horn slammed against your head is something you probably won't remember until later in the evening, after you wake up with a few stiches in your head!

Slip down on the inside of a spinning bull, and he'll jump away from you, making a recovery next to impossible. On a spinning bull, your safe escape has just become much more difficult. The bull will make you his target as he continues around in his spin. Take a bull head-on, and you're going to lose.

Once he knocks you down, he isn't going to stop. Having a hoof of a two-thousand-pound bull land on you is going to crush ribs and break bones.

Needless to say, I quickly learned where to focus during those long 8 seconds if I wanted any chance of making the buzzer and getting out of the arena alive.

There is a point between the bull's front shoulders where the hair starts—a cowlick of sorts. If you stay focused on that spot, you might have a chance.

If you focus on the bull's head, which is very hard not to do by the way, as most of them have long horns, you will not last long. The bull can throw his head to the left and go to the right. Your momentum and counter-move is headed left, following his head, and you will not recover when he goes right. That is why most riders focus their eyes on the bull's shoulders; he has to go where the shoulders go.

Maintaining focus may sound easy, but believe me, it's not. Remember in my last example when I rode Sanchez. As soon as I started listening for the buzzer, I lost my focus and was bucked off. Any loss of focus, regardless of the reason, will result in a No Score.

Milky Way

I remember drawing a grey Brahma bull named "Milky Way." Milky Way
was not that big, but he was fast. If you know anything about bulls, you
know you can recognize a Brahma bull by the small, camel-like hump on
his front shoulders.

Now remember what I just told you about focusing on the bull's shoulders? This bull's hump introduced a new problem for me. As I slid down
into the chute and onto Milky Way, I instantly realized there was nothing to focus on. Instead of the spot between his shoulders, I was staring
at a hump.

The hump is not made of bone but rather a large mass of muscle. It can
be pushed from side to side. When Milky Way bucked, his hump would
flop back and forth in the opposite direction he was going. What was I
supposed to focus on?

I set my rope and riding hand a little tighter than usual, slid up onto my rope, looked down, and nodded for the gate. Milky Way blew out into the arena, taking a long first jump. I instinctively focused on the point between the shoulders where my hand was tied into the rope. All I saw was a hump flopping from side to side. This was not going to work. I couldn't keep my head down.

On the second jump my focus shifted forward, but all I saw were horns. Experience had taught me to not focus there. I needed to find a spot somewhere else if I was going to maintain balance and ride this bull. I looked back down at my hand in the rope for something to focus on.

At this point, Milky Way was bucking in a straight line. I was in good shape and still in the center of his back.

The Ground Is Hard

Suddenly, Milky Way cranked it hard to the right, and I found myself hanging on the outside of the bull's spin. Instantly, I reverted to my physical strength, trying to pull myself back up on top.

The right counter-move would have been to relax and let the bull's momentum swing my body weight faster than his spin, bringing me back on top and into the natural rhythm of the ride. If this pattern were to continue and I were to use my natural strengths making the necessary adjustments, I might make the 8-second buzzer!

Well, I didn't do any of that. Milky Way jumped again, and by now it was too late. I felt the momentum sucking me off the left side of the bull's back. I pulled hard with my riding hand and dug my right heel into his side.

Milky Way felt my weight shift. He increased his speed to the right in a tighter circle. At 5.8 seconds the G-force was too great. My hand came out of the rope, and I was thrown clear of the ride.

I flew through the air, landing hard on my butt. My chin slammed against my chest when I hit the dirt, and I bit my lip. My back cracked from the impact. Needless to say, I was a bit dazed.

Milky Way stopped bucking the instant I hit the ground. He just stood there staring at me. Adding insult to injury, he slowly meandered out of the arena the ultimate victor. I sat there in the dirt, feet spread apart, my mouth bleeding, and watched Milky Way walk out of the arena. The crowd acknowledged my effort with a round of applause.

Getting Focused

Nothing gets your attention quicker than landing hard on the ground off the back of a bull. Lose focus and that will be the end result.

Not having focus leaves you vulnerable to non-value-adding activities—activities that really don't contribute much to the goal. When you lose your focus on the critical activities, you soon get consumed by the trivial and find your personal effectiveness hitting the ground early.

The 80/20 Principle, a book by Richard Koch, explains how using 80/20 effectively can keep you focused and accelerate your progress. The 80/20 principle teaches you to focus on the critically important 20% activities and to ignore the 80% activities contributing little or no value.

The principle states: 80% of your accomplishments will be the result of 20% of your activities; 80% of your sales will come from 20% of your customers; 80% of your customers will purchase 20% of your products, and so on.

Our days are full of interruptions. We focus on a 20% project and quickly find ourselves being pulled into a variety of less important 80% activities zapping our precious time.

We all have our favorite pet projects and activities we enjoy doing. These activities, however, may not be focused on our core 20% goal, but we enjoy spending time on them anyway. It is important to note that these activities may very well be important, but are they critical to you achieving your goal? Balance the time you spend on these less important activities, leaving plenty of time to focus on your 20%.

I experienced firsthand in bull-riding that when you lose focus on the important 20%, it isn't long before things start going south. This being the case, why is it so hard for us to stay focused on our 20%?

Why is it so hard? Because we don't differentiate the critical 20% activities from the trivial 80% activities. If everything has the same level of importance, we jump from activity to activity, never getting anything accomplished.

Identifying Your 20%

For the next few days, record all the activities you are involved in that take at least fifteen minutes of your time. Next, examine the list, and identify those activities that are obvious time-wasters. Remove them from your list.

Using the remaining important activities, carefully examine each one and decide if that activity is critical to achieving your balanced-thinking vision. Cross out any items that are or seem to be less important. If Koch is right (in my experience he usually is), 80% of your list will fall into that category.

Looking at the remaining activities, identify two or three that, if you could focus solely on them, the rest would become less important or be eliminated altogether. These remaining activities are your critical 20%.

Spend your time working on the critical 20%, and don't waste any more time working on the 80%. Once you have the 20% items completed, don't go back to the remaining 80% items.

You will find your remaining 80% activities have little or no relevance when the 20% have been accomplished.

What To Do With The 80%

The reason we do the exercise of identifying the critical 20% is to focus our attention on those critical activities that deliver results. The question comes up every time: What do you do with the 80% activities? You can't simply choose to ignore them. What if people, employees, or customers are involved in the 80% activities? Do you simply ignore them as well?

These are all valid concerns. But we must not get bogged down by non-value-adding activities. My response to these questions is to make your 80% activities *someone else's* 20% activities. Just because an activity doesn't make *your* 20% list doesn't mean it isn't important to the overall good of the organization. Pushing it down into the organization allows someone else to examine it against their 80/20 list. More times than not, it will make someone else's 20% list.

I have a client who is an Edward Jones financial planner. His office had achieved a level-three ranking and had been performing at that level for a few years. He identified his critical 20% as "self-employed individuals nearing retirement age." His expertise was creating exit strategies for these clients.

Having identified his 20%, as the principle teaches, every other type of client fell into the 80% category. Ignoring these 80% clients would give him more time to devote on the 20% clients.

Not wanting to simply send these clients away, he referred them to another Edward Jones financial planner whose critical 20% was a different demographic. In return, the other financial planner referred his exit-strategy clients back to him.

Because of his 80/20 focus, my client's business jumped from a level three to a level five in one year.

As you practice 80/20, you will have more time, and your work will become much more effective. Be careful here, though. Pushing down your 80% might imply that you want it done by a subordinate regardless of their personal 80/20 ranking. Teach and encourage your entire organization to use the 80/20 principle, and your organization will flourish as everyone focuses on their all-important 20%. Encourage everyone in the organization to eliminate the unimportant 80%.

One final note on 80/20. The absolute best use of your time focused on an 80% activity is in finding a way to give a less important 80% opportunity to your competition. Let them focus on the opportunities you don't want, and the result will be more 20% opportunities you do want. It takes discipline to turn away an 80% opportunity. Stay focused and it will result in a stronger financial bottom line.

Sacred Cows Make the Best Burgers

When you identify your critical activity list, those activities not categorized as a 20% get labeled as an 80% non-value-adding activity. What happens when one of these 80% non-value-adding activities is required by management or by an organizational process? When regardless of its

80/20 ranking, you are required to do it? I call these not-up-for-discussion activities *Sacred Cows*.

The book *Sacred Cows Make the Best Burgers* by Robert Kriegel and David Brandt addresses the topic of sacred cows. Sacred cows are those issues, processes, policies, individuals, and practices that for one reason or another are not up for discussion.

They become sacred cows for any number of reasons: *It's the way we have always done it. The process was developed by the Boss. Just do it, and don't ask questions. That's the pet account of the V.P. of Sales, and they play golf every Friday. By the way, don't ask about the pricing.*

You must deal with the sacred cows. As the title of the book suggests, *Sacred Cows Make the Best Burgers.* If you identify an 80% activity getting in the way of a 20% activity, you have to deal with it. These sacred cows are grazing *everywhere* in our companies; unless you have the courage to get them out into the open and deal with them, you will never achieve the ultimate goal of sustainability.

Attempting to make a burger of a sacred cow without the organization having a balanced-thinking vision, however, will end in disaster. The sacred cow will remain healthy and strong if there isn't a clear goal in mind that exposes the sacred cow as a constraint or roadblock to achieving the goal.

If you can't identify the sacred cow as a constraint to a 20% activity, then I recommend you ignore it. It won't cause any significant issue anyway. It isn't worth the effort or the time it would require eliminating it.

GETTING ON THE BULL
How To Focus on the Critical Issues

The third lesson is learning how to identify and deal with critical issues. Not dealing with critical issues is a significant contributor to poor performance. It consumes the time and efficiency of individuals, teams, and organizations. Not only do you need to distinguish between *critical* and *time-wasting* activities, you must decide what to do with them.

> *Deciding what not to do is as important*
> *as deciding what to do.*
>
> —Steve Jobs

Identify the critical issues. *You start by differentiating between the 20% critical activities and the 80% non-value-adding activities. Next you identify any sacred cows that may be grazing amongst your 20%. Get them out in the open.*

Stabilize the process. *When we eliminate non-value-adding activities from our processes, we create activity gaps. While this is a positive improvement step, you must stabilize the process to ensure the results continue to be achieved. Non-value-adding activities can be found in many areas of your business including sales, management, operations, supply chain, human resources, and information technology, among others.*

Drive issues to ground. *As we get further involved in the process of streamlining, i.e., closing the gaps, these issues must be driven to ground. Illuminate them, delineate them, and eliminate them, but don't ignore them. When we don't drive issues to ground, they reoccur at the most inopportune times.*

It will take some practice to identify the critical from the non-value-adding activities, especially if you have been doing them for a long time. Having a process to identify critical issues will help.

A simple rule-of-thumb for categorizing a problem as a critical issue is to determine if two or more of the following are true:

+ *The issue is related to a core organizational function.*

+ *The problem directly or indirectly affects a significant number of people.*

+ *The problem adversely affects customers and/or key stakeholders.*

A critical issue can be thought of as a problem or opportunity that is critical to the overall success of the organization.

Identify the Critical Issues

When identifying critical issues, you might find it helpful to consider the following questions:

1. **Why is this issue critical?** *It is important to fully understand an issue before we classify it as critical and energize the organization to solve it.*

2. **Who is this a critical issue for?** *What meets the criteria of critical for one individual might not meet the criteria for someone else. Are you attempting to address personal critical issues or organizational critical issues?*

3. **Is this a new issue or an old issue?** *If the issue is old, ask the next question: what was done about it before? It isn't unusual for organizations to solve the same critical issue repeatedly. Finding a solution that drives the issue to ground is the ultimate goal!*

4. **What, if anything, changed to make this issue critical?** *Sometimes we identify a new critical issue when we engage in the process of solving an existing one. Asking what has changed will help us understand if our work has uncovered a new issue, or is there something else causing it.*

5. Is the identified issue a sacred cow? *Understanding the differ-ence between a critical issue and a sacred cow before attempting to solve it could drastically affect the actions required to drive it to ground. Identify sacred cows early in the process to effectively eliminate them.*

This step of identifying critical issues requires patience. Don't get in a hurry here. Work cross-functionally to insure you gather all the available information about the identified issues.

Initially, you may find your organization tends to make all issues critical. Use 80/20 to identify the *most* critical issues. Having a balanced-think-ing vision will give you the reference you need to separate the 80% from the 20%.

Don't be intimidated. When you identify a critical issue, get it out into the open. You will never reach a stable business environment without addressing critical issues.

When a critical issue is identified as a business process, more effort will be required to deal with it. There are usually a lot of moving parts. When stabilizing a process, employ "USA"—Understand, Simplify, and Automate. This simple-to-remember process, when employed, saves companies millions of dollars a year by eliminating process complexity and non-value-adding steps.

There are two kinds of critical issues: the ones jeopardizing your prog-ress toward the goal (Bad) and the ones absolutely necessary to achieving the goal (Good).

The USA Process will assist you in eliminating the bad issues and focus-ing on or automating the good ones. Focusing on the critical drivers and eliminating the non-value-adding activities is the key to getting where you want to be.

Stabilize the Processes—USA

Understand:

Take the needed time to understand your critical processes. Don't automatically assume you know what is going on. Make sure you gather enough data about how the existing process performs in terms of performance, efficiency, and accuracy.

Simplify:

It is important to simplify the process as much as possible before you automate. Often manual processes evolve over time, so determine whether each step is actually necessary. Simplifying the process before automating it will ensure that the benefits of software and technology (automation) can and will be realized.

Automate:

The next logical step in business process optimization is to automate (or semi-automate) the business process. The most commonly understood benefit of process automation is that it saves labor. However, it is also used to save energy, materials, to improve quality, accuracy, precision, and to eliminate or minimize human interaction.

USA is a powerful tool once you have your organization focused on the vision. Understanding how your value-drivers create customer value and differentiation is extremely important to your long-term success.

Plus, as a process tool, USA can be applied to literally any balanced-thinking initiative you choose.

> *Example:* "I want to finish next year's Iron Man triathlon in less than eight hours." Apply USA and get to your goal.

Understand: *Identify your current habits and how they might be helping or hurting your progress toward running the Iron Man in under eight hours.*

> *Positive habits: riding your bike, eating healthy, and not drinking and smoking.*
>
> *Negative habits: oversleeping, eating at restaurants, and Starbucks' Iced White Chocolate Mocha.*

Simplify: *Eliminate all the non-value-adding activities distancing you from your goal. For USA to be effective, you have to do the work. So long, Iced White Chocolate Mocha!*

Automate: *Having eliminated all the non-value-adding activities, create a daily routine that includes the positive habits needed to be ready for the Iron Man. Expand it to a weekly routine and then a monthly routine. Automating your activities eliminates the need for deciding each day how you are going to get there.*

Focus on understanding the critical issues, simplifying the process, and automating to get repeatable results. When it comes to dealing with the critical issues and the sacred cows, drive these issues to ground. You don't want them coming back.

Drive Issues to Ground

The step of *driving issues to ground* is one of my personal favorites. It is so effective in turning a company around that if you do nothing else, this step will dramatically improve your performance.

Getting others to speak up is extremely important when getting to the root of a problem. You must create a safe environment by encouraging everyone to express their points of view and then work together to resolve them.

Ask *Why?* five times. Developed by the Japanese for Kaizen (a business improvement methodology), asking *Why?* five times allows you to drill down to discover the root cause and effect of a particular problem. Each *Why?* question forms the basis for the next question.

Asking *Why?* five times encourages collaboration between teams. Problems are rarely isolated to one function or team. Engage subject-matter experts across the organization to work together when resolving complex problems.

Asking *Why?* five times brings additional resources to a situation. When problems cross boundary lines, the intensity to resolve them diminishes. "It's no longer my problem." In extreme cases, you might want to consider external resources to focus on a specific issue and eliminate finger-pointing.

Issues rarely get fully driven to ground. We simply don't take the time required to resolve them completely. Unfortunately, that means they will be visiting us again.

Don't ever be satisfied with solving the immediate concern and moving on, assuming you will finish the job later. You will never get back to it. It is extremely important to sustainability to eliminate these non-value-adding activities before moving on.

Ask Why? *Five Times.*

Example: When having a learning conversation

1. You ask: *How are things going today?*
   They respond: *Fine.*
   (*"Fine" is always the answer by the way.*)

2. You ask: *How do you know?*
   They respond: *Because engineering hasn't been out here all day.*

3. You ask: *Does engineering spend a lot of time out here?*
   They respond: *All the time, especially since we changed vendors.*

4. You ask: *Is there a problem with the vendor we are now using?*
   They respond: *Seriously? You haven't heard?*

5. You say: *No. What's the problem?*
   They respond: *If they aren't late, most likely they have made it wrong. They really struggle with getting it right and on time.*

That may not be exactly how your questioning will play out, but asking multiple, well-thought-out, intentional learning questions will uncover much more than if you didn't spend the time really communicating.

By asking Why? five times, you not only discover a significant issue needing attention, you develop a relationship with an employee on a much deeper level.

Eliminate All Non-Value-Adding-Activities

Identify the 20% activities you need to spend time on. You need to meticulously understand what it is you do daily that provides value for your clients.

When your list of value-adding activities is complete, start working on your ability to execute those activities. Invest in these activities with people, training, process development, and automation. Remember, these activities result in 80% of your current and future success.

Eliminate activities that do not add value. These are the time-wasting activities/processes you need to *remove*. Eliminating time-wasters is a continuous task, and the more effectively you work at it, the more time you will have to focus on value-adding activities.

Automate the value-adding process, the 20% activities that, when streamlined, can be automated, minimizing the human input requirement. Insure repeatability over time by automating critical, value-adding processes.

When you remove non-value-adding activities, make sure to capture the financial value of the improvements. You can realize improvements in the areas of cost reduction, delivery cycle times, overall human interaction, and improved customer satisfaction.

A benefit rarely considered when removing non-value-adding activities is employee morale and job satisfaction. The employee morale meter will improve when you eliminate activities eating away at their time, allowing them to focus on tasks that really matter.

FOCUS ON
CRITICAL ISSUES
Eliminate all Non-Value-Adding Activities!

+ *Identify the Critical Issues*
+ *Stabilize the Processes*
+ *Drive Issues to Ground*

CONCLUSION

Balance, focus, and counter-moves are what it takes to ride a bull for 8 seconds. Focusing on and implementing the 20% activities are what it takes to grow a sustainable business. With a balanced-thinking vision clearly in front of you, now is the time to identify the critical activities, processes, and practices required to make it a reality.

Identify the 20%, ignore the 80%, deal with the sacred cows, and drive issues to ground. Like a bull rider, these are the counter-moves needed to keep you centered and on target. Don't forget to push through your intimidators and to act.

Distractions are everywhere, and it will take focus to stay on task. Work on it daily, reviewing them at the end of each day to see how well you did. Don't get discouraged.

When you can, move your 80% activities down, making them someone else's 20% activities. When an activity is not worthy of your 20% list, shifting it to someone else's 20% list gives them the opportunity to step up. It allows them to do something you would have normally completed. It will help them stretch and grow, accomplishing what is now a 20% for them.

Help others with their 80/20 exercise. You know the saying—"it all runs downhill." By continuing to identify the 20% at all levels while eliminating the 80% creates a streamlined, focused organization.

Focus is the only way to maintain balance on the back of a bull. Get focused, identify the critical issues, and deal with the sacred cows.

FOCUS ON CRITICAL ISSUES
The third lesson of Boardroom Bullrider

BOARDROOM BULLRIDER

LESSON 4

CLOWNS
DEVELOP KEY RELATIONSHIPS

Understands the importance of relationships and that companies
don't make decisions, people do. People do business
with people they know, like, and trust.

PRE-ASSESSMENT:
DEVELOP KEY RELATIONSHIPS

❏ You've developed strong relationships with key individuals critical to the success of the business.

❏ You consciously maintain these relationships through regular face-to-face meetings and events.

❏ You have a documented, concise, and effective process for setting goals and evaluating and rewarding employees.

❏ The organization is comfortable giving and receiving feedback and is willing to learn from one other.

❏ There is an overarching, unspoken culture within the organization to *have each other's back.*

❏ You encourage and provide opportunity to celebrate individual, team, and organization achievements.

The Strength: _____

The Weakness: _____

The Opportunity: _____

The Threat: _____

If you can't ask more
of your relationships,
you're left to
fend for yourself —

Everyone loves the clowns. That's a big part of why we go to the rodeo. To see the clowns. Clowns play an important role in the overall rodeo experience. They provide action-packed, entertaining stunts that please the crowd during the down time between events. They wear baggy pants, suspenders, and colorful shirts. Their job is to make us laugh. They use dog tricks, sheep acts, and horse-riding stunts to keep everyone entertained.

However, when the bull-riding starts, rodeo clowns take on an entirely different role, that of a *bull fighter*. The laughing stops. Everything gets serious as they transform into the bull riders' best chance of surviving an event. Without bull fighters, bull riders wouldn't live to tell their tale.

The role of a bull fighter during the bull-riding event is twofold: 1) help the cowboy score as many points as possible and 2) get the bull rider out of the arena unharmed.

Bull fighters try to turn the bull into a spin during the ride to increase its intensity. When a bull rider is thrown from the back of a bull, the bull fighter's job is to put himself between the bull and the rider—to do whatever it takes to distract the bull long enough to allow the rider time to get out of the arena.

Then there is the barrel-man. This bull fighter stands in the center of the arena with a barrel during the bull-riding event. The barrel is brightly colored to attract the bull and is padded on the outside for the bull's protection and on the inside for the bull fighter's protection.

The bull fighter places the barrel directly in the path of the bull. He stands around it, on top of it, and inside it, hoping to attract the bull his way. If he can get the bull to charge the barrel, he'll jump inside to avoid a direct hit from the bull. The barrel goes flying, or in some cases rolling, across the arena with the bull fighter nestled tightly inside.

Sounds like a great job, right? Bull-fighting clowns are well-trained athletes. Most spectators don't realize the number of skills they possess.

The Professional Bull Fighters (PBF) exists to help train bull fighters, to hone their skills at working the bulls and assisting riders. They compete for prize money and to win the title of the best bull fighter in the business.

The PBF has identified some judging criteria that are critical to become a world class bull fighter:

+ **Turning Bulls Back:** *The ability to engage the bull to make him turn back and spin, if needed, to gain the rider more points.*

+ **Dismount Positioning:** *To be in the right place when the bull rider dismounts takes precision timing and a great deal of bull savvy. The bull dictates where the bull fighters will be at all times during the ride. The bull fighters must be able to react instinctively to the bull's actions to be able to give the bull rider the best possible opportunity to escape unharmed.*

+ **Hooking Prevention:** *The bull fighters analyze not only every move the bull makes but the rider, too. By doing so, many times the bull fighters can prevent the wreck before it happens by spotting little things that cause the bull rider to be bucked off and possibly hooked. Sometimes, there is nothing they can do to prevent the injury but are engaged in the wreck, distracting the bull to give the bull rider a chance to escape.*

+ **Hang-Ups:** *When the bull rider gets hung up, the bull fighters will work as a team, with one getting the bull's head under control while the second bull fighter goes to the rider's hand and works to free it from the rope.*

+ **Degree of Difficulty:** *The danger factor of not only the bull, but also the situation. A horned bull that hooks will have a higher degree of difficulty than a muley (no horns) bull that hooks. Many times the difficulty lies in the situation the bull rider is in, such as a hang-up, where the bull fighters have to expose themselves to more risk.*

- **Aggressiveness:** *The bull fighters' aggressiveness to the action taking place during and after the ride.*

- **Showmanship:** *The ability to take the situation and make it entertaining for the audience.*

Bull fighters are gutsy, fearless guys who are extremely fast on their feet. They have to be able to turn on a dime to miss the horns of a charging bull. This is extremely dangerous as the bull fighter will step in front of the charging bull, grab the bull by the horns and attempt to steer him away from the rider. You can only imagine the potential for injury.

Did I mention fearless? I once saw a bull fighter jump right onto the bull's head, sitting right between the horns like he was riding on the handlebars of a bicycle, all in an attempt to distract the bull and to get the bull rider to safety. They will do whatever it takes when called upon to do so.

It's a critical partnership between the rider and the clown. It's about knowing and understanding fully the job at hand, anticipating potential hazards, and doing your part to achieve a successful ride. Clowns are every bull rider's best friend. These guys should never buy their own beer.

A Bull Named Tiger

I was riding a bull at the Southeastern Idaho High School Rodeo Regional Finals held in Salmon, Idaho. I had drawn a bull named "Tiger." Aptly named, he had the coloring of a Bengal tiger. Not a terribly difficult bull. Certainly one that I *should* have been able to ride.

As it is in bull-riding events, a lot can go wrong on even the easiest bulls. Maybe I was looking past this one. Maybe I wasn't focused. Needless to say, I quickly found myself in a bad situation.

It was the final event of a three-day rodeo. I had qualified for the finals and drew Tiger as my bull. I wasn't too concerned about riding him. I had seen Tiger buck earlier in the week. A straight bucker and, if the clowns did their job, maybe a few turns. It wouldn't be a high score, but if I rode him, I should place in the top five.

It was an afternoon event. The bull-riding is always last, so it was still early in the evening. It was early June, and the night was warm and comfortable. The stands were still packed as everyone had stayed in their seats to enjoy the finale.

Tiger was already in the chute, so I slid my rope around him, tied it off, and climbed out to wait my turn. I would be the fifth bull rider called. I watched as the four riders before me attempted their bulls. No 8-second rides yet. Now it was my turn.

I slid back down on Tiger and got busy setting my rope. My mind was calm as I handed the tail of the rope to my riding buddy and slid my hand in the loop. He pulled the rope tight.

Tiger was a bit uneasy in the chute. He was leaning heavily against the gate, pinning my leg. I took my wrap, pushed my hat down, and got ready. I paused for just a moment before nodding for the gate and attempted to get Tiger to stand up straight. He wanted out, so I nodded my head.

The big gate swung open, and Tiger blew out into the arena. As we left the chute, my foot slid against the gate, pulling my foot back and me out of position. My body twisted, sliding my hips sideways.

The first jump is critical. It sets the timing for your counter moves and can determine the outcome of the ride. Coming out of the chute wrong or having your timing behind the bull's usually ends in a no score. With my foot hitting the gate, my timing was well behind the bull on this one.

With all the arm strength I could muster, I pulled on the rope, throwing my foot forward in an attempt to get back into position. By now Tiger was a full jump ahead of me. As I landed back up on my rope, his massive head went down, and his back feet kicked high into the air. I felt my body hinging on my wrist like a teeter-totter.

The force pushed me out over the front of the bull. I threw my free hand back and pulled my knees up, trying to overcome the force, but my moves were of no avail. I was not going to catch up to him.

I found myself sort of in a Superman position on the back of Tiger with both of my legs flying behind me. My body was being slammed around with every move this bull made. I knew it would be impossible to regain a riding position. All I could do was attempt to get off safely. It all happens so fast, within a couple of seconds.

When you decide it's time to eject from the back of a bull, it's not like you have a lot of time to think about it. With my free hand, I grabbed wildly for the tail of the rope. Luckily, I found it and pulled hard. My riding hand slipped cleanly out of the rope.

Good News, Bad News

Good news, my hand was free from the bull rope and Tiger. Bad news, I was now airborne. Tiger's next jump came exactly at the same time I was attempting my dismount. I flew through the air over the bull's head, diving straight down to the ground directly in front of the bull and under his hooves.

I landed head-first and rolled into a ball. The impact forced the air out of my lungs, and I was unable catch my breath. I was in the wrong place! I knew I was in big trouble.

At that very instant, from out of nowhere, I felt a hand grab the back of my pants and pull me out from under the bull. The entire ordeal must have looked choreographed, like one smooth, fluid movement. However, to me it felt as if I had just been in a motorcycle accident, hitting the pavement at sixty miles per hour.

The clown had been running alongside Tiger, entirely aware of my situation, grabbing at my belt while I was still in midair. As soon as I hit the ground, he pulled me out and away to safety.

I rolled over as quickly as I could, only to see the bull and the clowns running the other way. I slowly got up, gasping for breath. Hunched over, I slowly walked out of the arena, still covered in dirt and disappointed with my performance. I had let this one get away. The crowd was cheering, so I assume my attempt was a bit of a crowd-pleaser.

I don't know what could have happened that day in Salmon, Idaho. But I do know it all worked out okay because of the skill, guts, and determination of a bull-fighting rodeo clown.

This would not be the last time I would escape injury because a clown was exactly where he needed to be when I needed him to be there.

Develop Key Relationships

We have all been told at one point in our lives to work on developing relationships. We must have taken this advice seriously. Social media platforms like LinkedIn, Facebook, and Twitter, to name but a few, are proof that we value relationships. As bull-fighting rodeo clowns are to a bull rider, there are vital relationships in your life that are essential to your achieving your goals.

With your balanced-thinking vision solidly in place, your intimidators and critical issues identified, you now can ask yourself, *who are the important people that are vital to my success?* Reach out to them, and start or strengthen your relationship with these people. Increase your networking activities if you can't identify key individuals. One thing is certain—you can't do it alone.

When developing key relationships, look for individuals with talents you don't have, talents vital to your achieving your goal. You want to build relationships with people who have an assortment of skills and talents who can augment the skills you already have.

I heard a story told by a multi-million-dollar lottery ticket winner who, when upon discovering he was holding the winning ticket, hired a tax attorney, a banker, a financial investor, and a public relations manager. All skills he would soon need and didn't possess himself.

A note of caution: We tend to gravitate to people who think like we do. Those who have the same interests and opinions. These relationships are great when playing golf or going fishing, but not when looking for help with a key initiative.

Personality profiles like DiSC®, Meyers Briggs, and Strengths Finder 2.0 can be useful when building your team to better understanding how they are wired.

Example: While working with The Corporate Core of Boulder, Colorado, I was introduced the Core Clarity model shown below. If you are heavy on the Reflect side and don't connect well with others, look for individuals who lean toward the Connect/Mobilize side. They will help get your ideas formed and communicated. You also might want to seek out individuals who lean toward the Mobilize/Energize side. They will help turn your ideas into action.

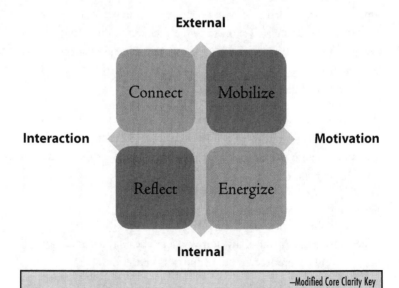

—Modified Core Clarity Key

Balance the team's capability, and build strong relationships. These key individuals will make all the difference. They are your bull-fighting rodeo clowns.

Social Media

Building relationships has changed radically in the past decade. Technologies like the Internet, smartphones, and social media have changed how we communicate and socialize with one another. These devices help us share ideas and experiences, stay in touch, and communicate around the world when forming and maintaining relationships.

At the same time, if we rely on technology too much, it may prevent us from developing the essential relationship qualities and skills that allow us to make real connections and build genuine relationships. Putting forth the time and effort of a one-on-one will result in a relationship you can count on. Invest in face-to-face opportunities when developing your key relationships. The value is extremely important and fulfilling.

> *It troubles me that we are so easily pressured by purveyors of technology into permitting so-called 'progress' to alter our lives without attempting to control it—as if technology were an irrepressible force of nature to which we must meekly submit.*
>
> —Hyman G. Rickover,
> Polish-American naval officer

That was in 1986. I imagine what he might say now!

Develop a balance between technology and face-to-face. Technology eliminates the problem of distance and has made the world a very small place. But it has also made our communication very public and impersonal. You don't develop deep, meaningful relationships in a text message or e-mail.

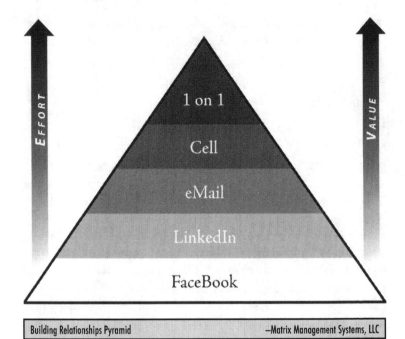

| Building Relationships Pyramid | —Matrix Management Systems, LLC |

Once you have identified those key individuals who are important to your success, get to know them face-to-face. Invest the effort of a one-on-one. The value of relationships increase as we make the effort to invest in each other. Then—and only then—use technology and social media to share events and to maintain your relationships.

Later on, I talk about asking more from your relationships. For this to happen, you must invest up-front to enjoy the benefits of strong relationships later.

Make and Keep Agreements

In the book *First Break all the Rules* by Marcus Buckingham and Curt Coffman, an in-depth study is conducted on what the world's greatest managers do differently. The book is a result of observations based on

80,000 interviews with managers as conducted by the Gallup Organization. It was one of the largest studies of its kind ever undertaken. One of the important points I took away was the discussion on why people leave organizations. Why do people quit? Understanding the answer to this question would prove to be extremely important in my future turn-around work.

What Buckingham and Coffman say is that the number-one reason people quit their jobs is because of their relationship with their direct superior. They don't respect their boss. It's not money—it rarely is. It's not the work or the hours. The most stated reason people quit is that they don't get along with their boss!

What I have experienced in more than 20 years of working in and with professional relationships is that most of the time relationships get strained by a lack of trust, i.e., our lack of making and keeping agreements. This lack of making and keeping agreements has contributed to more broken relationships and disgruntled employees than any other single issue.

Talk More—Assume Less

In the book, *The Four Agreements* by Don Miguel Ruiz; the third agreement states: "Don't Make Assumptions—Find the courage to ask questions and to express what you really want. Communicate with others as clearly as you can to avoid misunderstandings, sadness, and drama. With just this one agreement, you can completely transform your life."

The problem is, *We don't talk*! We hide behind hidden agendas, false or unrealistic expectations, and unfulfilled promises. We think if we talk openly, we might be exposed or we run the risk of being misunderstood. We stop our conversations short and assume the other person knows what we meant and what we expect.

We have all been there. You start a new job and are left with the expectation of a first-year performance review. Raise your hand if you got that expected performance review on your anniversary date. That's what I thought. How many of you got the review at all? Unfortunately, this agreement is broken most often in companies experiencing trouble.

I find it more prevalent with employees in middle management positions. They fail to receive an effective review from upper management positions, their boss, so they don't see the value of providing effective reviews for their direct reports. You can't build key relationships on broken or unfulfilled agreements.

We make agreements all the time. Too often, however, we make the leap from stating the requirements to expecting the results. The *4-R's of Making and Keeping Agreements* will drastically increase your chances for success.

The 4R's of Making and Keeping Agreements   —Matrix Management Systems, LLC

The 4-R's of Making and Keeping Agreements

Requirement: *Unless we clearly identify the requirements we have of each other, we shouldn't expect the results to be accomplished.*

Responsible: *Who is responsible for what? Don't leave it to chance or assume they know. Make sure everyone is aware of what he or she is agreeing to do.*

Resources: *Don't assume everyone or everything needed to complete a project will be readily available. Chances are, some of the critical resources won't be.*

Results: *We do what we are inspected to do. Following up with a team member or an employee isn't a bad thing. Don't consider it imposing or looking over their shoulder. It shows you care, are engaged in the process, and care about the results.*

When you make an agreement, clarify that you are, in fact, making an agreement. Identify the requirements for each member involved. Define who will be responsible for what. Ask if everyone is in agreement. Get a verbal acknowledgment to ensure you actually have an agreement.

And don't stop there. Define the resources needed to keep the agreement. You can't keep your agreement if the key resources required aren't available. Meet often to check up on each other, keeping the desired results in view. Accountability is key. The best way to develop accountability in an organization is by making and keeping agreements.

Your life works to the degree you keep your agreements.

—Werner Erhard

GETTING ON THE BULL
How To Develop Key Relationships

The fourth lesson is developing key relationships. All relationships are important. But when the outcome of an initiative relies on a key individual, that relationship becomes vital. Developing key relationships to ensure an outcome is realized is a responsibility you must focus on.

Whether you are using social media or meeting someone face to face, you must find ways to enlist them in your initiative, engage them in the process, and secure a relationship that will last.

Identify key individuals. *Identify those individuals who are vital to your initiative or goal. Ask yourself, what skills, experience, and relationships are going to become vital to your success? Without these key relationships, your chance of success is questionable. Enlist their help.*

Build trust and credibility. *When building trust and credibility with a key individual, the most important step is listening. Ask for their help, then listen intently. Try not to think about what you're going to say next until you have processed what the other person has just said. Slow the conversation down and show some respect. It's not about you!*

Ask more of your relationships. *The most important assets you have are your relationships. You invest a significant amount of time developing, cultivating, and maintaining them. When these relationships are vital to your initiative, don't be afraid to ask more of them. If you have followed my advice, they will be eager to help in your cause. They are easily engaged and will want to be all in. Remember the team-player-choice model in the first lesson.*

What helps us to be the best leader we can be? Engaging in authentic, learning conversations to explore new ideas. Ask genuine questions and allow the other person sufficient time to answer. To ask great questions, you need to listen carefully and craft a question that does not elicit an obvious answer.

Engaging in learning conversations forces you to look beyond the obvious, to analyze, assess, learn, and make decisions. This will demonstrate your expertise and enhance credibility.

Once you have captured your balanced-thinking objective, eliminated your intimidators, and identified your critical issues, cultivating vital relationships is the next step.

Identify Key Individuals

There is nothing more important and vital to the human condition than good relationships. Possessions can be lost or taken away, but a good friendship can last forever.

You know when you have met someone of significance when you realize this person enhances instead of complicates your life—when you see them take a personal interest in your well-being, putting you first in the relationship.

Maybe you have experienced this type of individual. I'm not referring to a spouse, sibling, or parent. These enlisted relationships exist for a completely different set of reasons. I'm talking about friends and associates that have a choice to be "fully in" or to "step out" from time to time.

If you want to build vital relationships, identify with whom and why. What does this individual have that is critical to your success? Be honest in your request and enthusiastic when soliciting their help. Offer to reward them for their effort. Show that their participation is vital. Respect their advice.

Slow your conversations down when talking with key individuals. Ask the kind of questions that will deepen your understanding of each other.

Open up a bit, allowing yourself to be exposed. Show you trust them and they can trust you.

I can't stress this next piece of advice enough: do your homework! Know as much about this key individual as possible. If this is a first meeting, make sure you get it right. First impressions count. Don't flood the conversation with your request for help. Take time to build the relationship. If you want to build an extraordinary relationship, give it time.

If it is an existing friend you are trying to enlist, be genuine and ask for their help. Most of us are willing, even excited to help when asked. Be genuine in your request and generous in your reward.

What you should strive for is to have better than normal relationships—truly extraordinary relationships with these vital individuals. What you really want to have is a superior relationship.

Trust and credibility are based on how you communicate with others and how you follow up on that communication. Your ability to build trust and credibility is crucial to maintaining vital relationships. Lack of credibility—how believable you are—can cause others to withhold trust.

Build Trust and Credibility

All lasting relationships require trust and credibility. Without it they wither and die.

I recently saw an interesting list titled *50 Ways to Lose Trust and Credibility* by Frank Sonnenberg. Here are my top 10 favorites from his list:

1. Act nice only when you need something.
2. Claim to be an expert in everything.
3. Fail to follow up promptly.
4. Adopt a messy physical appearance.

5. Show up late or miss deadlines.

6. Compromise your principles and values.

7. Expect others to do what you wouldn't do.

8. Accept credit when it's undeserved.

9. Make rules but don't follow them.

10. Run from tough decisions.

I'm going to practice and be careful not to allow these types of activities to creep into my key relationships. I hope you do too.

When you follow your own advice, you build trust and credibility in your relationships with friends and colleagues, not to mention respect from your peers and employees.

Take a self-assessment by asking yourself these questions:

Do I keep confidences? *When people trust you, they're most likely going to share confidences. Keep them to yourself. Trust can take a long time to develop and a moment to destroy.*

Do I accept feedback gracefully? *When you ask for someone's opinion, honest feedback may feel risky and difficult. Even if you don't agree with his or her assessment, welcome it with an open mind. It will improve your credibility.*

Do I follow up on people's concerns? *Listening to people's concerns is helpful. But be prepared to make those changes or explain why you can't. Never leave their concerns unaddressed.*

Do I practice damage control? *Be extremely careful of what you say when times are difficult. One slip can do irreparable damage to your credibility. If you slip, take immediate steps to repair the damage.*

It takes years to build trust and credibility and an instant to lose it. When developing key relationships, you understand the value of trust and credibility. You invest additional effort to ensure you are understood and you understand others.

When relationships reach this deep level of understanding, trust, and credibility, you can ask for favors. Both of you will want to help the other. You can ask more of your relationships, having confidence in the result.

People do business with people they know, like, and trust. Companies don't make decisions, people do. Asking more from your relationships can open doors for you that otherwise could not be opened.

For better or for worse, it's not just what you know or are capable of; it's who you know that's important. You can learn a tremendous amount from people in your network who are willing to share their experience and expertise.

Ask More of Your Relationships

Have you ever asked someone, "Is there anything I can do for you"? and hoped they'd say no? When they say, why yes, you think to yourself, I wish I hadn't asked.

I work in a volunteer organization where a monthly visit is required. We try to visit every member monthly to ensure that everything is going well with them. It has become customary just prior to leaving their home to ask, is there anything I can do for you?

Many a time, I have been on the receiving end of that question, only to see the person squirm when I pause for just a moment to give it some thought. Then I get to watch their relief when I say, "No, we are good."

If you are going to ask more from your relationships, you need to be willing to put in the effort first. I have been on the receiving end of relationships when the needed help arrives without my asking. They were aware and concerned enough to provide the assistance without being asked. This type of relationship enhances your life. It doesn't complicate your life regardless of which side you are on, the giving or the receiving.

Most of us are not very good at asking for help or advice. Let me offer a few suggestions I have found helpful over the years.

Be honest and straightforward. *Don't be afraid to tell others what you are dealing with. If you clearly express your need, you'll find that most people will empathize with you and be willing to help.*

Don't feel overly guilty or entitled. *Find the balance between feeling guilty and entitled. Maintain a positive attitude when asking for help, and don't expect everyone to simply jump in. Most important, make your needs clear—don't beat around the bush.*

Asking for help can serve as a favor to someone else. *People honestly feel better about themselves and their relationships when they can provide useful service. Genuinely show your appreciation, and they will be more likely to help next time.*

Be ready to reciprocate. *I owe you one is a common phrase used after someone provides us service. Look for opportunities to pay it back with meaningful activities.*

Stay in touch. *When others provide assistance, share with them the result of their effort. Sometimes the outcome of their assistance won't be fully realized until much later.*

I have a business colleague writing a book on sales titled *Ask for the Cookie*. The best salesmen in the world understand the importance of inviting someone to help or asking someone for the order. How often do we forget to ask? Don't be afraid to ask for help. Asking more of our relationships will get us what we want and need.

As I close out this chapter, let me talk for just a minute on accountability. When developing key relationships, accountability is a must to maintain trust and credibility.

Accountability is one of the most important aspects of any relationship. A company that reinforces and holds its employees accountable for the choices they make and the tasks they perform achieves high levels of productivity and efficiency.

Accountability, or the lack thereof, is a popular topic when working in a troubled company. It is a nail in the coffin if you don't have accountability among your leadership. Lack of accountability will find its way deep into your organization and take a great deal of effort to get back.

The biggest deterrent to accountability is the lack of understanding, the making and keeping of agreements. Make sure that, before people leave a meeting, expectations are clear, ownership has been defined, resources are identified and committed, and measurements and reviews are set.

Then empower your employees to deliver. When employees don't feel empowered, they lack the flexibility and freedom to act on their own. Instead, they continually seek your approval prior to taking every necessary step.

Accountability is always realized when others understand their role and how they contribute to the overall goal. Defining everyone's expectations up front insures understanding of what's expected.

Reinforce accountability in every activity, function, transaction, and service you perform. Never allow yourself or anyone else to not be held accountable. It's simply too important.

As you've heard me and others say before, you can't get there alone. I learned this lesson over and over each time I slid down onto a bull and nodded for the gate.

DEVELOP
KEY RELATIONSHIPS

Make and Keep Agreements.

+ *Identify Key Individuals*
+ *Build Trust and Credibility*
+ *Ask More of Your Relationships*

CONCLUSION

In bull-riding, rodeo clowns taught me the importance of building key relationships. Thirty years in business have taught me the importance of keeping key relationships strong by making and keeping my agreements.

Remember that you can't go it alone. Make and keep agreements with key individuals to maintain a strong relationship, and they will help you achieve your goals.

Making agreements, while critically important, is something most of us don't do very well. Slow down, learn to listen, and most important, make verbal agreements. When you do, you will get the results you seek.

Earn trust by investing in your relationships. Don't rely solely on social media. Invest in one-on-one time. Social media tools are great when maintaining a relationship, but not to build, repair, or advance a key relationship.

Finally, ask more of your relationships. Fully expect them to engage in your vision. Be accountable, and make sure you reciprocate when asked. They might very well be asking more of their relationships too.

Who are your rodeo clowns? Develop key relationships, and maintain them by making and keeping agreements.

DEVELOP KEY RELATIONSHIPS
The forth lesson of Boardroom Bullrider

BOARDROOM
BULLRIDER
LESSON 5

SELF-PRESERVATION
BUILD A SUSTAINABLE ORGANIZATION

Provide a path or process in a positive, sustainable direction
to enlarge, develop, or expand beyond the current state
that minimize defects and deliver value.

Pre-Assessment:
Build a Sustainable Organization

❒ The current business model structure can achieve the budgeted financial targets.

❒ There is sufficient knowledge of the market and the competitive landscape.

❒ The critical activities that create differentiation and value are identified and mapped.

❒ The current market opportunities are leveraged and tracked with metrics.

❒ The company maintains updated market intelligence from various sources, both internal and external.

❒ You possess the ability to develop and expand into competitive markets.

The Strength: _____

The Weakness: _____

The Opportunity: _____

The Threat: _____

When a business
can't survive without you,
it won't—

Sometimes, regardless how well you plan, things just don't go your way. This is especially true in bull-riding. Regardless of how well you prepare, one wrong move and you'll find yourself in the dirt with an angry bull bearing down on you. In those moments of panic, you realize just how fast things can go wrong.

If you are one of these unfortunate individuals who have experienced a bad day, and I mean a really bad day, you know what I am talking about.

One moment all is well, and you are enjoying your surroundings. Then, in a split second, all hell breaks loose. You get blindsided by a bus you never saw coming.

> *Self-preservation is the first law of nature.*
> —Samuel Butler, an English author

It's in our nature to want to survive. In these unfortunate moments, we learn to appreciate the power of self-preservation.

I've seen bull riders get slammed to the ground, dragged through the dirt, and then stomped on, only to jump up, run to the fence, and climb over to get out of the arena. Two steps outside of the arena they collapse in a pile, totally unconscious to the fact that they did this all on a broken leg.

I can honestly say each time I climbed on the back of a bull, I felt this self-preservation mode kick in. I expect it can be said of other extreme sports as well—that sobering moment when you realize you could get hurt, maybe even killed, you push past the desire to stay safe and nod your head. Crazy as it sounds, you just go for it.

Ringo

During the rodeo circuit's off season, a local stock contractor operated a ranch in Rexburg, Idaho, where he had built an indoor arena. He kept some of his bulls there for the winter. To stay sharp, we would ride his bulls for fun and to get some off-season practice. To make things interesting, we would each put twenty bucks into a hat and hold a winner-takes-all event.

It was on one of those cold winter days in Idaho that I drew a large, rank bull named Ringo. Ringo was taller than most bucking bulls, and with my being taller than most bull riders, it was a good match.

This indoor arena was much smaller than the standard outdoor arenas. Because of the smaller area, the bulls were more apt to buck in a circle—what bull riders call a "spin." This made for good practice. It's much harder to ride a spinning bull than one that doesn't spin.

There were eight of us bull riders looking for a good time, so we rounded up eight of the best bulls. It was a bitter cold day, and you could see the bulls' breath as they entered the holding pen. Needless to say, this made them look meaner, adding to the intimidation factor.

Ringo held back as four bulls were pushed into the chutes. While waiting my turn, I helped the other cowboys and watched as they bucked their bulls. Ringo ran into the chute, and I quickly slid down on him. I had to take my coat off to make the ride, and I could feel my muscles already getting stiff from the cold.

He was a big bull, and my legs were pressed tight against the chute. The chute was made of steel; the metal was cold against my legs. Ringo must have been feeling the cold as well. He stood quietly while I pulled my rope and got set.

I nodded my head for the gate. Ringo's first jump was slow as he headed into the arena. Quickly, we reached the far side. Ringo hit his full stride as he cranked it hard to the left, into my hand. When the bull turns into your hand, you have a better chance. You can rely more on arm strength and less on balance and counter-moves.

Ringo continued in his left-hand spin. I kept focused on his shoulders and my next counter-move. The arena was tight, so Ringo stayed in the spin for the full 8 seconds, like a massive dog chasing his tail. My timing was on, and I was able to keep up with him.

I had made the buzzer but the spinning ride had put me in a bad position. Although I had worked hard to stay centered on Ringo, I had slipped down into the inside of the spin. I had overcompensated.

When the bull feels you sliding into the spin, he widens his rotation. The force away from the center of the spin pulls you down into the middle of the vortex. Bull riders call this "sliding into the well."

And yep, while riding Ringo, I slid down into the well. Now—trust me when I say this—it is a very bad place for a bull rider to be. As the bull continues to spin, you're directly in his path. Landing in the middle of this tornado, you stand a very good chance of getting horns, head, and hoofs—in that order. Lucky for me, Ringo didn't have horns, but I found out his head was just as hard.

Ringo came around lowering his head, hitting me squarely in the chest, pile-driving me hard onto my back. I was looking up at his front hooves flying over my head. I knew his rear hooves would be coming down right on top of me. My self-preservation instincts kicked in, and I pulled my knees to my chest, trying to cover. As Ringo planted his feet, they brushed my head, landing on my hat, covering my face with the cold dirt. I felt the rush of his hooves as they brushed my face.

My self-preservation mode was now in high gear. I rolled over to get out of the way. No longer under Ringo, I jumped to my feet. I couldn't see. My eyes were watering and full of dirt. I couldn't make out the chutes, so I just started running. I knew, given the small arena, Ringo would be quickly coming around again. After a few stumbling steps, I found the fence and climbed over. I had made an 8-second ride, but getting off had nearly ended in disaster.

Glad To Be Alive

In bull-riding, this self-preservation mode proves very useful. It can mean the difference between life and death. In business, however, I discovered there is a second type of self-preservation mode. I call it the "self-ish-preservation mode." It's the desire to promote one's own agenda, one's own progress, one's own career. This tendency, unfortunately, comes at the expense of other people.

That day on Ringo was the closest I ever came to getting badly hurt while bull-riding. I escaped injury, but there was a split second when I found myself in serious danger. I remember to this day how that felt. You don't have time to think—just react. I remember covering up my face, bracing for the impact. Lucky for me, it never came.

Of the five Boardroom Bullrider lessons, Lesson Five will be the most difficult to master, because diminishing your ego is counter intuitive for almost all of us.

I have observed the selfish-preservation mode occur during a difficult interview with an employee. When the individual feels his or her job might be in jeopardy, the selfish-preservation mode kicks in, and the discussion gets intense. If not managed properly, it can become confrontational and jeopardize a good employee and a great learning opportunity.

Here is another example. I observed this selfish-preservation mode occur when I challenged a senior management team member to consider getting some outside help because the business initiative he was championing had started to founder. This business leader unfortunately viewed it as a threat to his personal credibility rather than an opportunity to help him and the company improve.

The organization continued to struggle, and the opportunity slipped away. His selfish-preservation mode took over, and in the end, everyone lost.

Learning to recognize and manage selfish-preservation instincts will open doors that are not available to you when your guard is up.

> *When we quit thinking primarily about ourselves and our own self-preservation, we undergo a truly heroic transformation of consciousness.*
>
> —Joseph Campbell, an American mythology professor, writer, and orator

It's Not About You

Selfish-preservation is a bad thing when working in an organization that is trying to create something special. It can mean the difference between poor performance with the lack of accountability and the objective of realizing a sustainable result. Our natural instinct of selfish-preservation must be kept in check to allow the organization to realize its full potential.

The easiest way to say it is, *It's not about you!* When we do or create something great, our selfish-preservation mode kicks in and we want the world to know that it was all about us. *We* did it. It was *our* great idea that turned the tide.

If this is where your selfish-preservation ego lies (and with most of us, unfortunately, it is), I would ask you to consider making an adjustment. *It isn't about you.* It's about understanding the circumstances that enable your existence—what is actually happening to create your success. It's rarely just about us.

Why were you successful? What conditions or events were present that allowed you to achieve the success? Who were the people (what vital relationships) who helped you along the way? If we consider our accomplishments this way, we gain a better appreciation and understanding of the process of success, rather than just basking in the glory of our achievement.

To create a sustainable organization, we must create an environment or culture of success—one that celebrates the collective contribution, not just our own personal awareness and capabilities.

Why is Lesson Five: "Self-Preservation," so vitally important? Because it's the key ingredient to creating sustainable value.

Creating Sustainable Value

In my career, I have been involved in a number of acquisitions. I have come to realize there are two lies told in every acquisition: 1) Nothing will change, and 2) we want the management team to stay.

As for "nothing will change," for a company to successfully transition to new ownership, changes are inevitable. Cultures need to mesh. Processes need to realign. Employee expectations must be satisfied. Expect *everything* to change, and you won't be disappointed.

As for "we want the management team to stay," this is almost always a temporary declaration. Acquired management teams have a difficult time transitioning into the new culture. However, it's extremely important for them to stay long enough to help the acquiring organization through the initial transition.

I have experienced this all too often. An *it's all about me* business owner wants to transition his business, only to realize *he is the business*, and without him his business isn't worth anything.

The fact is, we are all temporary. If you want to build something of value, it can't be about you. It doesn't matter if we are talking about your family, your organization, or your business. You will exit someday, and the goal should be to create sustainability. Build a high-value organization capable of continuing long after you are gone.

When selfish-preservation is driving your actions, you diminish value. It's all about me. You may be extremely successful in your selfish-preservation role. Many of us are. You may want to take a vacation sometime, maybe play a round of golf on a regular basis or create a highly valued business. If so, you need to create an organization that is self-reliant and self-learning.

Remember, it's not about you!

Be-The-Paper

Sustainability is about developing processes that deliver value. Understand that your critical processes are key. One way I have helped companies accomplished this is through an exercise I created during one of my turnarounds. I call it *Be-The-Paper*.

Be-The-Paper isn't complicated. Simply write your name and a product or service you provide on a sheet of paper. Select something that's required to go through a number of steps or processes to create or execute.

If it makes more sense, create an actual order or follow a customer's order through your process. The important point is you are going to track, monitor, and record every step, process, and time when the order is resting.

Now follow the paper. Ask your employees to treat the order as they would any other order. When it moves, you move. Record the actions required to complete the order. This is called a Process Map.

Try to stay out of the process as much as you can. Capture the times when the process requires your attention. Identify ways to minimize your involvement.

I had a client use Be-The-Paper to reduce their order-entry time down from two weeks to twenty-four hours. It was powerful to see the process in real time and to observe the amount of non-value-adding activities the employees were able to remove.

Develop, educate, and automate your organization to function without you. We will cover what you should be working on later. For now, work on getting yourself out of the day-to-day activities.

Be-The-Paper will help you **understand** how your organization creates value—value your customers are willing to pay for. Value which differentiates you from your competition.

Once you accept your role as a leader is to create sustainable value, go to work gaining a deeper understanding of how your operation really works. Compare it with your competition, and identify ways to increase differentiation. Identify the critical steps your organization employs in its processes.

Process-Map these critical steps, educating your organization on the importance of the work they are doing, driving the company forward.

Next, we **simplify** these value drivers. We want to eliminate waste. We don't want to apply resources on activities that produce little or no value. These are our 80% activities. Remove all non-value-adding activities from the process.

Another important activity when simplifying any process is to measure the results of our work. Identify the value, impact, and importance of every step along the path. Assign a financial value to it; decide if it is critical. Capture and communicate the amount saved by eliminating non-value-adding activities.

Finally, we **automate.** Take the variation out. Insure repeatability. Minimize human interaction. Guarantee customer satisfaction.

Never apply Automation before the steps of Understand and Simplify. When you deploy software or other forms of automation without streamlining your processes, the result is a bad process now made more complicated.

The process of automation encompasses a variety of possibilities. The goal is to take as much human interaction out of the process as possible.

Be-The-Paper is an exercise in USA! (Understand, Simplify, Automate)

Sustainability

Remember I said *It's not about you?* It's not about *them* either! It's about minimizing or eliminating errors, getting a repeatable process.

Once you have invested in the work of USA, you want to ensure it stays that way. After the work is accomplished, we can wander off back into the weeds of complexity. It's not that we are lazy; we simply get focused on other things and take our eye off the ball. It doesn't take long for complexity and non-value-adding activities to creep back in.

Self-preservation as a bull rider can mean the difference between winning and being carried out on a stretcher. When self-preservation turns to selfish-preservation, we stop creating and start diminishing value.

Remain vigilant and watch for the non-value-adding 80% activities creeping back into your processes. Focus your efforts on creating and maintaining streamlined processes, value-driven activities, and long-term sustainability.

GETTING ON THE BULL
How To Build a Sustainable Organization

The fifth lesson of the *Boardroom Bullrider* is to create sustainability, learning to suppress our selfish-preservation tendencies. If you make it *all about you*, then *you* are required in order for the organization to be successful. You as an individual are not sustainable. You are a human, and, unfortunately, you are temporary.

Our selfish-preservation tendencies drive us to want to make it *all about us*. If we want a company or organization to flourish and thrive over time, we must create processes that are sustainable.

To ensure long-term sustainability, the foundation must be solid. You can't rely on the skills and talents of a few key individuals. People are temporary. Create processes that deliver results that when the talent pool changes, as it most certainly will, you can continue to deliver un-interrupted results.

Process-map critical activities. *Don't become complacent thinking you understand how your company's processes work. They change over time. Having a Process Map not only deepens your understanding of the current process, it provides a measured point-in-time to refer to.*

Measure your current capabilities. *Do you have the capability to accomplish your vision? You may have the talent, but do you have the time and the financial resources? Many initiatives are dead before they start because the organizational capabilities are insufficient to produce the desired outcome.*

Anticipate growth constraints. *Companies can get into trouble just as fast from too much growth as from not enough growth. Anticipating*

and preparing for growth has a unique way of bringing growth op-
portunities to fruition. If you want to grow, anticipate your constraints
and prepare for it.

As a side note, this Boardroom Bullrider Lesson should serve as the agenda for your company's next strategic planning meeting.

As you begin the work of developing a sustainable business model, develop a Process Map for clarification and for a deeper understanding of your value-adding steps.

Process mapping is a way to gain an understanding of your business processes and activities at a detailed level. This activity will identify and help to create a sustainable competitive advantage.

Process mapping of critical activities reveals the organization's core processes and how different parts work together to serve customers.

Process Map Critical Activities

The first step in any process-improvement activity is to understand the major elements, i.e., inputs and outputs, decision points, critical steps, and functions. Once you have a clear roadmap of the process, eliminate those activities that are non-value-adding, those that do not provide value. Put your customer hat on and ask yourself if you would be willing to pay for this step in the process? If not, it doesn't add value, so get rid of it!

Next, identify those critical activities that create differentiation and value for your customers. Value drivers can come in many forms, such as technology, delivery, aftermarket service, brand recognition, and satisfied customers.

Defining which *best practices* truly add value reinforces your communication efforts both inside and outside the organization. Create Key

Performance Indicators (KPIs) driving those critical activities deep into your organization's culture.

Process mapping provides a diagram of how the company provides value to its customers. Having a big-picture understanding of the business reinforces vision, defines strategy, and aligns employees' understanding on how their work reinforces the overall goal.

Process mapping can answer these questions: Is our business structured correctly? How do we deliver on our value proposition? These are both inward-looking activities.

Once you are certain you're operating at an optimum pace with your current products and services, you are free to look outward and explore new growth opportunities.

Measure Current Capabilities

Measure your current capabilities as you consider how and where your growth will come from. Don't underestimate the requirements of growing and expanding into new markets.

Healthy revenue and profit margins are crucial to any company. However, monitoring your bottom line is only one part of the formula. It's essential that you determine the factors critical to your company's success, i.e., your current capabilities.

Measure those metrics, and put into place a system for continually improving performance. Before investing in new markets, products, and/or relationships, consider the following:

Leverage your talent. Norm Smallwood and Dave Ulrich wrote in the June 2004 issue of *Harvard of Business Review*: Competence comes as leaders buy (acquire new talent), build (develop existing talent), borrow (access thought leaders through alliances or partnerships), bounce (remove poor performers), and bind (keep the best talent).

It is important that you become good at leveraging your talent. Getting the right people in the right seats on the bus is only the first step. Getting them to build processes around the incredible work they do creates long-term organizational sustainability. Make process-building part of their job description.

Develop your capabilities for change. *Measure how long it takes you to identify, define, delegate, implement and realize, change initiatives. Execution capabilities are critical in our ever-changing business environment. Your job is to keep your eye on the horizon and leverage your employees' talents to take you there.*

Be good at making and keeping agreements. *No, be great at it! Accountability is only considered a capability when the organization realizes it is unacceptable not to make and keep agreements. This capability starts with you. Be impeccable with your commitments. Never, and I do mean never, allow yourself or your senior management team to slip up here. Remember, everyone is focused on what you consider important, what is critical, and what is simply unacceptable.*

Be good at working cross-functionally. *Be capable of leveraging talent across the organization regardless of their functional area. Leveraging the talent pool when needed can be extremely effective at gaining efficiencies measured against competition.*

To achieve a sustainable organization, you must remember, it's not about you. Developing a company that is self-reliant and self-learning is paramount.

Anticipate Growth Constraints

Unexpected events always come at the most inopportune time, interrupting even the best-developed plans. Adept leaders identify and prepare for events that could interrupt or constrain implementing their business growth plan.

These events are referred to as constraints. That is, events that significantly interfere with executing the plan. You should consider which constraints are likely to be encountered and what steps can be taken in anticipation of these constraints.

Get an unbiased, formal assessment of the competitive landscape. This information, when accurate, will provide the timing, product features, and pricing for market entry opportunities.

Identify a defensible value proposition. Understand what you are exceptional at, what you bring to the market, and why customers would want to buy from you.

Ensure that all your resources and capabilities are in alignment. When experiencing rapid growth, critical resources are at a premium. Resource-constrained organizations must align everything. Leverage your talent on those critical activities that drive customer satisfaction.

The most important thing you can do as a leader is build passion and commitment. Inspired organizations produce inspired results. Leaders must be continuously out front, modeling the way by overcoming obstacles, communicating vision, measuring accountability, and building trust and credibility.

Never rush into a new opportunity without fully vetting the potential constraints. I have witnessed companies rushing in to take advantage of a hot new opportunity only to have the hot new opportunity bring them to their knees. Unfortunately, it usually comes at the expense of the core business.

BUILD A SUSTAINABLE ORGANIZATION

It's not about You!

♦ *Process Map Critical Activities*
♦ *Measure Current Capabilities*
♦ *Anticipate Growth Constraints*

CONCLUSION

Self-preservation is a good thing when escaping an enraged bull that has just slammed you to the arena floor. It can mean the difference between pain and injury and escaping unharmed. Our instinct for self-preservation when in danger drives us beyond what our normal capabilities would allow.

Selfish-preservation restricts an organization working to create something special. It can mean the difference between poor performance with the lack of accountability and the organization realizing a sustainable result.

Give the USA process a try and see if you can streamline your value-adding-activities. Apply automation to ensure that, over time, you maintain the results you worked so hard to get.

Eliminate as much human interaction in the processes as possible, reducing the possibility that when personnel changes are made, the integrity of the process isn't jeopardized.

Know your business' value drivers by process-mapping critical activities, measuring current capabilities, and anticipating growth constraints. Drive customer differentiation by understanding the key factors that set you apart.

Finally, give your organization the opportunity to achieve the vision by your getting out of their way. Having a well-communicated, balanced-thinking vision, identifying and working on your intimidators, having dealt with the critical issues and sacred cows, and leveraging key relationships, your need to be in front of your team is minimized. They are empowered with the tools for achieving the goal.

Self-preservation is important in bull-riding for getting out of a bad situation. Keep your selfish-preservation in check, and remember it's not about you. The goal is to create a sustainable organization.

BUILD A SUSTAINABLE ORGANIZATION
The fifth lesson of Boardroom Bullrider

If you can't let go,
you become
part of the problem—

BOARDROOM BULLRIDER

BONUS LESSON

BOTTOM-UP LEADERSHIP
GET OUT OF THEIR WAY

Leadership is most often interpreted as top-down— a position in a hierarchy, layers of management, and levels of responsibility.

Bottom-Up Leadership is similar, not that the hierarchy is reversed, but whomever is responsible allows subordinates to assume a greater role in critical decision-making supported by established processes, procedures, and clear communication.

BOTTOM-UP LEADERSHIP PYRAMID

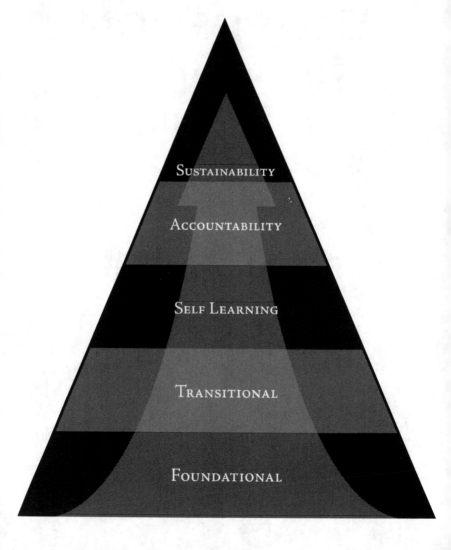

Having learned the Five Lessons of *Boardroom Bullrider*, you now recognize the ultimate goal is to create sustainability. Sustainability is developing an organization capable of continuing on long after you're gone.

When working in and with companies going through the Five Lessons, a successful implementation requires the management team to let go of some of the activities traditionally done at their level. Working in the business isn't a productive use of their time anymore. Basically, they get in the way.

Once the Five Lessons are implemented, your need to micro-manage is no longer a 20% value-adding-activity. You will undo all the good work you have done if you can't step back and allow the organization to do what you have taught it to do.

In the beginning, implementing the Five Lessons was a 20% activity for the management team, requiring 80% of their time, energy, and focus. Your job was to identify and communicate the vision and to set the example by *modeling the way*. At this point in the implementation process, the management team needs to transition to a different 20%.

Bottom-Up Leadership is about working on your 20% while the organization works on its 20%. What are your new 20% activities, you ask, now you are no longer needed to work in the business? You desperately need to find the answer to this question, or you will drift back into your old, comfortable routine.

Your once-needed daily routine of answering questions and giving directions, stepping in to solve the toughest of problems, and teaching the organization how to perform are no longer a priority. By now they are well equipped to handle it on their own.

Your new role is one of organizational support, providing the team with the necessary resources for them to execute their way up the Leadership

Triangle. Give them what they need for each level, and get out of their way! Here is a list of supporting activities you should now be focusing on:

Communicate the vision. *Communicating the vision moves the organization from 'Foundational' activities into the 'Transitional' phase of the Bottom-Up Leadership Triangle. Maintaining a constant message and modeling the way reinforce the vision and insure a smooth transition.*

Celebrate short-term wins. *Celebrating short-term wins reinforces 80/20 and the need to focus on value-adding activities. Through your ongoing reinforcement of these aptitudes, the organization becomes 'Self-Learning'.*

Unleash your talent. *Give people room to grow, take risks, and create their own metrics. They become accountable when working to achieve a standard they themselves set. You will have reached a level of genuine 'Accountability' when they hold themselves and other team members accountable.*

Reaching the top of the Bottom-Up Leadership Triangle, your organization is "Sustainable". It now has the potential of continuing on long after you are gone.

Bottom-Up Leadership is about creating a process that involves intentionally bringing people together to contribute to a positive vision based on deeply held values. It is also about action planning so people are prepared to actively work toward what they envision.

Companies that practice Bottom-Up Leadership with a clearly communicated, widely understood, and collectively shared vision have been shown to outperform those who don't.

Communicate the Vision

All participants must share the same vision for change, one that includes a common understanding of the problem and a cooperative approach to solving it. Ensure that every member of the organization has a process to measure their personal daily, weekly, or monthly contribution to the overall goal.

Identify organizational KPIs as a shared measurement system. Collecting and measuring KPI results not only ensure that all efforts remain aligned, they also enable the participants to hold one another accountable and learn from one another's successes and failures.

Provide consistent and open communication across the organization to all stakeholders to ensure trust, reinforce objectives, and provide the motivation needed for realizing the vision.

It is a good practice to identify individuals to be the cross-functional implementation team for the entire initiative. This team will coordinate the efforts, provide clarification when needed, and insure team alignment for achieving the vision.

As you reinforce direction and model the way, it's time to celebrate. Everyone likes to win. Make milestones meaningful and special. Show your appreciation for the work the organization is doing. Encourage your team to continue to step up.

Celebrating short-term wins builds momentum and enthusiasm for the change initiative. Honest-to-goodness, tangible evidence the change effort is making progress is essential.

When you celebrate short-term wins, you create urgency and spur on momentum toward the goal. Even with a balanced-thinking vision, you still need tangible proof that progress is being made.

Generate Short-Term Wins

Select milestones that represent unmistakable improvements driving the organization toward the goal. There should not be any debate that the vision is producing and will produce the desired results.

People need to see real, tangible progress toward the goal to validate the change process. When you achieve a short-term win, make sure the organization celebrates it and the win doesn't go unnoticed.

Ideally, short-term progress results should start to appear within 90 days. Organizations get distracted with other 20% activities like customer needs, competition, and employee issues when the goal is too far into the future.

Ensure that short-term milestones are relevant to the majority of your stakeholders. If they don't see the connection to the overall vision, they will not fully support the efforts required to achieve it.

Short-term wins should provide a test of the vision, an opportunity to measure the potential of the identified result. They should be convincing milestones for fully realizing the vision of the desired future state.

Don't allow your organization to get stagnant. Celebrate and raise the bar. Celebrate improvement, not consistency. Even when consistency is the goal, look for ways to decrease cycle times, reduce cost, or increase value in an already consistent process.

Never get behind. The pace will always get faster, and you will never catch up. Remove all encumbrances to success. Unleash your talent by letting go and getting out of the way.

Unleashing your talent means removing all encumbrances and roadblocks from your talented people. Allow your people to best utilize the skills and capabilities they possess to get the work done.

Basically, you must contribute to the vision and provide the required resources, then get out of their way and let the talented people be successful. To unleash your talent, alter your normal activities of ask, direct, and require and adapt a new approach of encourage, support, and provide.

Unleash Your Talent

Leaders must state it plainly and simply: "We welcome, even encourage your ideas, passion, and talents." Identify individuals who have untapped talent and are eager and willing to step up to a higher level of accountability.

Provide the required resources to model and test their ideas. Develop a process for measuring an idea's potential, requiring a short financial analysis of the benefits. This will not only further develop your unleashed talent, but provide a platform to self-eliminate non-value-adding ideas.

When unleashing your talent, be clear about where you need help to achieve the vision. Welcome new ideas and encourage people to explore opportunities on their own. They may well go home and return with the answer.

Require your up-and-comers to identify educational opportunities for improving their overall effectiveness. Pay for these courses when successfully completed to build, encourage, and nurture your talent. Don't get cheap—this investment will pay big dividends.

Your new role is now clearly visible. You are at the helm, guiding the organization as it executes initiatives with precision. Employees are accountable, and morale is at an all-time high. You have become the company to work for.

Whether your company is focused on Customer Intimacy, Product Leadership, or Operational Excellence, as discussed in *The Discipline of*

Market Leaders by Michael Treacy and Fred Wiersema, you will be required to expand and change.

Few markets, with the exception of Wheaties and Cheerios, have remained unchanged. Leaders must be able to envision new opportunities to grow and expand their organizations. Done correctly, this aptitude will prove invaluable to your sustainability.

What Are Your New 20% Activities?

Understanding your marketplace. *Understand its past and current trends and when and how they occurred. Don't rely solely on employees' opinions. Make the effort to contact key customers, competitors, and suppliers, looking for indicators of future trending opportunities. Do the work!*

Check your analytics. *Every IT professional will encourage you to analyze your website data. The signs of emerging market opportunities are already present. Your analytics can pinpoint opportunities providing you with the most educated expansion moves possible.*

Identify lagging market opportunities. *Being first to market may sound great, but in reality, it is risky and can be very expensive. Once one or two companies have proven the market, it might be a great time to jump in, addressing the obvious issues the early providers haven't.*

Identify the second bounce of the ball. The Second Bounce of the Ball *by Sir Ronald Cohen is a book about identifying market opportunities before they become obvious trends.*

Identify opportunities with "second-bounce" potential, and you may be more likely to enter new markets at that most critical and opportune time. The greatest example of this concept is Apple's iPhone. Talk about hitting the market at the most critical and opportune time!

Bottom-Up Leadership isn't for everybody. You have to stand back and step out of the arena. It will be hard to let others do the work. Your selfish-preservation mode will kick in as you harbor feelings of being sidelined.

Focus on the aptitudes of Bottom-Up Leadership. Master the art of modeling the way. Teach your organization how to celebrate wins, and unleash your talent. Enjoy what you have built.

Now get back to work!

It will take a constant effort on your part to reinforce all that you have learned. Never take your eye off the prize.

BOTTOM-UP LEADERSHIP

Get Out of Their Way!
- *Communicate the Vision*
- *Generate Short-Term Wins*
- *Unleash Your Talent*

CONCLUSION

The next generation of leaders is well on its way to changing how we do business. Don't tell them they can't do something…or worse yet, that it can't be done! Unleash these up-and-coming individuals on your problem, vision, or goal, and watch what happens.

It's okay to establish some ground rules and to identify those few non-negotiables that you simply are not comfortable changing. But once this is done—get out of the way!

I have to say it again: Drive the 80/20 principle deep into your organization. Encourage the elimination of non-value-adding activities. Teach your organization how to focus on their 20% activities. The next generation is easily distracted by technology and social media. Leverage it where you can and manage the rest.

Keep your vision clearly out in front for all to see. Be consistent in your communication and your modeling of the way. Make your celebrations of short-term wins impactful and meaningful.

Don't celebrate when they come close to meeting their goals or simply because they *tried really hard*. Celebrate when it is deserved: *when you win*! These up-and-comers were raised in a generation of participation trophies. That might work in Little League, but not here.

Unleash your talent on newly envisioned markets. Watch how they develop the necessary skills to gain momentum over the competition. They will hold themselves accountable for the results.

Get on the bull, get yourself set, pull your hat down, and nod your head. It's going to be an amazing ride!

Develop the Foundational Bottom-Up Leadership style by Transitioning to Self-Learning, Accountability, and finally achieving Sustainability.

BOTTOM-UP LEADERSHIP
GET OUT OF THEIR WAY
The Bonus Lesson of Boardroom Bullrider

BOARDROOM BULLRIDER

PROGRESS ASSESSMENTS
HOW FAR HAVE WE COME?

People do
what they are
inspected to do.—

When I was riding bulls, there wasn't such a thing as video replays. There really wasn't any way I could have seen how I looked during the ride. More important, there wasn't any way of seeing what I did wrong.

I relied on others to give me feedback on what to do better next time—really not the best way to improve.

I listened to what they told me and compared it with what I had just experienced. In the end, I just got on another bull and hoped for the best. My balanced-thinking enthusiasm provided the courage needed to give it another try—always telling myself, "You got this!"

When our enthusiasm is high, knowing we are firmly in the driver's seat, we develop an *I Got This* attitude. We strengthen our *I Got This* attitude every time we experience success. Most of the time it's a good thing; it drives us forward when times get tough. It drove me to get on that next bull.

There are those times, however, when our *I Got This* attitude isn't good. It's when *I Got This* turns into ego and consumes our thoughts. We begin to think we are invincible. It's in these moments we can mistakenly take ourselves, and unfortunately others, down the rocky path to trouble. Our ego-driven *I Got This* attitude gets in the way of our success.

Stop Lying to Yourself

I have experienced the ego-driven *I Got This* attitude in a number of leaders. Their organizations are in chaos, and they continue down the path with their ego flying high. They go around spreading the good word of everything is fine, while those around them know full well things aren't as rosy as they are being portrayed.

While giving a *Boardroom Bullrider* presentation at a management team's monthly staff meeting, one attendee said, "I didn't know we were broken!" A few weeks later, the CEO was fired for lack of performance.

How could the staff have missed the impending firing of their CEO? All the signs were there: poor financial performance, no desire for cross-functional teamwork, low employee morale. The culture had deteriorated. There was a lack of communication, and employees complained about inconsistencies across the organization.

Were they lying to themselves, or were they truly unaware of just how bad it really was? Was it the old tale of the frog in the pot?

Frog in The Pot

You are likely to know the story about the frog placed into a pot of luke warm water. The frog rests easily in the pot of water, enjoying its surroundings. If the water is then heated slowly, according to the tale, the frog won't jump out but remains in the pot, eventually getting cooked by the boiling water.

The moral of the frog story goes something like this: Letting small and seemingly harmless wrongs slip could kill or at the very least be bad for you. Basically, it encourages us to not be complacent but to be observant of seemingly minor changes that may be harmless at the time but can become serious if left unattended.

There is a way to predict when the temperature in your *I Got This* pot is slowly rising—a way to identify the critical areas that need attention. It's really quite simple—ask!

Assessments

There are many ways to ask. One of the best ways, if you want to know the specifics about your critical activities, is to craft an assessment. With a series of well-crafted questions, you can learn a lot about your organization. Don't let your ego-driven, *I Got This* attitude boil the frog.

Assessments are an important step in finding out where you are, how you are doing, and what you need to improve on. In some cases, you discover new information. Yet most of the time, assessments validate what you already know. When you are honest with yourself, you usually know where you are slipping and what you need to work on.

The "I didn't know we were broken!" statement made at the company staff meeting was simply that individual ignoring the obvious. He knew they were in trouble. He fully understood the outcome of ignoring the signs. Unfortunately, I have witnessed this problem too many times. They choose to ignore the problem, or refuse to admit it even exists when, in reality, it will never go away. It will only continue to get worse.

The *Boardroom Bullrider* Progress Assessment will answer the following questions: Where are you currently? How are you progressing?

Modern day bull riders, like other professional athletes, watch videos of their performance. You are no different. Assess your progress and make the necessary adjustments to achieve your goal of sustainability.

TRACK YOUR PROGRESS
Assessments from Boardroom Bullrider

The Five Lessons in *Boardroom Bullrider* will take you to your balanced-thinking vision. Like bull-riding, you must stay balanced and focused. Counter-moves are required to make the 8 seconds.

How are you doing with your ride? Is your vision compelling? Have you removed intimidators? Are you focused on the critical issues having removed the sacred cows? Are you developing key relationships? Finally, have you gotten out of the way—or is it still about you?

Take the Progress Assessment at least once a year and measure progress toward you vision. It will keep you on track.

Progress Assessment
Lesson 1—Creating a Compelling Vision

Rank each statement in the post assessment from 5–1;
5=Strongly Agree, 1=Strongly Disagree.
Maximum possible points for this post assessment is 30

_____ *The company's vision is an inspiring statement of our desired future. It is clear, understandable, and well-communicated.*

_____ *I can see a clear linkage between my work, my groups' priorities, our customers' needs, and the company's vision.*

_____ *Time is allowed for envisioning projects, to include defining tasks and establishing deliverables and milestones required to meet the objectives of the project.*

_____ *When envisioning products, processes, and opportunities for improvement, cross-functional input is solicited from others, both internally and externally.*

_____ *When projects are identified, it is clear there has been sufficient effort to understand and communicate the value, impact, and importance of the initiative.*

_____ *Envisioned projects and initiatives for execution move smoothly from management to organizational oversight once milestones and key measurables are defined.*

_____ Total Lesson 1

PROGRESS ASSESSMENT
Lesson 2—Eliminate Your Intimidators

Rank each statement in the post assessment from 5–1;
5=Strongly Agree, 1=Strongly Disagree.
Maximum possible points for this post assessment is 30

_____ The leadership is clearly onboard with the vision for the company, deliberate about how to achieve it, and fully engaged in the work.

_____ The organization operates efficiently and effectively when conducting meetings, defining initiatives, and maintaining organizational alignment.

_____ A clear plan of action is communicated to the organization, defining how to align individual activities to achieve the goals.

_____ The company has clearly established strategic objectives that align priorities and marshal resources in the most efficient and effective manner.

_____ Activities are always measured; if the results don't meet company standards, the process is altered to achieve organizational goals.

_____ A minimum number of established Key Performance Indicators (KPIs) undergo a regular review process and are communicated across the organization.

_____ TOTAL LESSON 2

PROGRESS ASSESSMENT

Lesson 3—Focus on Critical Issues

Rank each statement in the post assessment from 5–1;
5=Strongly Agree, 1=Strongly Disagree.
Maximum possible points for this post assessment is 30

_____ *Before starting any project or process improvement initiative, the organization has open dialogue to identify critical issues and other potentially difficult roadblocks.*

_____ *Leaders reinforce the process by working through any and all impediments, regardless of their nature, to insure a clear path and to create alignment.*

_____ *Critical processes are regularly reviewed and actions taken to understand, simplify, and automate activities where possible to minimize errors.*

_____ *Expectations for tasks, projects, and initiatives are clearly understood, allowing for the most effective and efficient use of employees' time and talents.*

_____ *There is a structure in place that identifies tasks and milestones, communicates the progress, and encourages the organization to celebrate successes.*

_____ *When activities are identified that are not part of the critical 20%, they are removed wherever possible, reducing their impact on organizational effectiveness.*

_____ TOTAL LESSON 3

PROGRESS ASSESSMENT
Lesson 4—Develop Key Relationships

Rank each statement in the post assessment from 5–1;
5=Strongly Agree, 1=Strongly Disagree.
Maximum possible points for this post assessment is 30

_____ *Managers regularly engage employees in conversations to explore new ideas and different ways of thinking or to simply get feedback on key issues.*

_____ *A new-hire orientation process exposes and trains new employees regarding company agreements, business ethics, and principles.*

_____ *Guidelines are established to make and keep agreements and to facilitate a requirement to adjust, redefine, and get back in agreement when necessary.*

_____ *A strong willingness to support, encourage, and deliver on all agreements is in place to honor and respect the impact our agreements have on others.*

_____ *A genuine desire exists for management, peers, and others to listen, keep confidences, accept feedback, and follow-up on individual concerns.*

_____ *The company reinforces and holds its employees accountable for the choices they make and the tasks they perform.*

_____ TOTAL POINTS LESSON 4

PROGRESS ASSESSMENT

Lesson 5—Build a Sustainable Organization

Rank each statement in the post assessment from 5–1;
5=Strongly Agree, 1=Strongly Disagree.
Maximum possible points for this post assessment is 30

_____ *The company has a validated business model that has been verified with current, internal, and external market intelligence.*

_____ *Constraints that are likely to be encountered while implementing the company's strategy are anticipated, and proactive steps are taken to remove them.*

_____ *There is a culture that is clearly identified with the goal of driving behavior, developing habits, and creating results.*

_____ *There are examples of our culture interwoven into how we conduct ourselves, create value, and treat our customers.*

_____ *The critical activities that create differentiation and value for the company are identified and mapped for clarity and understanding.*

_____ *There's an ongoing effort to determine the critical factors for the company's success, and there are initiatives to build and develop those capabilities.*

_____ TOTAL POINTS LESSON 5

BOARDROOM BULLRIDER
SCORE CARD

_____ *TOTAL POINTS LESSON 1*

_____ *TOTAL POINTS LESSON 2*

_____ *TOTAL POINTS LESSON 3*

_____ *TOTAL POINTS LESSON 4*

_____ *TOTAL POINTS LESSON 5*

_____ *TOTAL PROGRESS ASSESSMENT POINTS*

BOARDROOM BULLRIDER
SCORE CARD

150 — 120	8-second Ride
119 — 90	6 Second Ride
89 — 60	4 Second Ride
59 — 30	2 Second Ride
Below 30	HIT THE DIRT

Maximum possible points for all post assessments—150

BOARDROOM BULLRIDER
BRAGGING RIGHTS

Bragging rights
are reserved for those with vision
and courage to explore
their potential——

My Grandpa Fullmer on his horse, Apache

Wrap It Up

Growing up on my Grandfather's Wyoming cattle ranch was a wonderful experience for me. For those early memories, I will be forever grateful. While working the cattle, I learned the lessons of hard work, appreciating what you have, and being accountable for your actions.

My path in life took me to the rodeo arena, where I was intrigued by the bull riders. Making the decision to get on my first bull was a never-look-back event. It forever imprinted on me the desire to give it my all, to push through even the toughest of circumstances with courage and perseverance. I owe much of my success in life to the lessons I learned during those 8-second rides.

I consider myself a visionary. I enjoy thinking about what could be and encouraging others to do the same. I know what it feels like to experience something that you dream of doing.

I hope you will venture out into the unknown, experience something great, and come home with some bragging rights.

Speaking of Bragging-Rights

On the following pages are some of my bucket list dreams I have experienced along the way. I hope to realize many more!

Scuba diving in Cancun, Mexico

Snowboarding Whistler Mountain, British Columbia, Canada

Flying a sail plane over the Flatirons, Boulder, Colorado

Riding a bull for 8 seconds, Afton, Wyoming

Having experienced these dreams, writing this book was my next great adventure. It has truly challenged me, and it was an amazing experience. I hope you read and follow *Boardroom Bullrider's* lessons and make your dreams a reality.

Draw a name out of a hat—put your hand in the rope—spurs in—hat down tight—and nod your head for the greatest 8 seconds of your life!

References

Books

Covey, Stephen. *The 7 Habits of Highly Effective People*

Kriegel, Robert and David Brandt. *Sacred Cows Make the Best Burgers*

Treacy, Michael and Fred Wiersema. *Discipline of Market Leaders*

Koch, Richard. *The 80/20 Principle*

Ruiz, Miguel. *The Four Agreements*

Magazines and Periodicals

Morris, Simon and Glenn Llopis. "A structured approach to problem solving." Forbes.

Biro, Meghan M. "5 Steps to Unleash the Power of Your People." Forbes. August 26, 2013. https://www.forbes.com/sites/meghanbiro/2013/08/25/5-steps-to-unleash-the-power-of-your-people/#56be02f42180

Kania, John and Mark Kramer. "Collective Impact Model." Stanford Social Innovation Review. 2001. https://ssir.org/articles/entry/collective_impact

Ulrich, Dave and Norm Smallwood. "Capitalizing on Capabilities." Harvard Business Review. June 2004. https://hbr.org/2004/06/capitalizing-on-capabilities

Whitbourne, Susan Krauss Ph.D. "Four Ways to Ask for, and Get, Your Favors Granted, If you want a favor from someone, you just need to know how to ask for it." Psychology Today. Feb. 15, 2014. https://www.psychology-today.com/blog/fulfillment-any-age/201402/four-ways-ask-and-get-your-favors-granted

Mattingly, Christopher. "Creating, Implementing, and Managing Effective Metrics." BA times. August 7, 2012. https://www.batimes.com/articles/creating-implementing-and-managing-effective-metrics.html

Archambeau. Shellye. "Cultivating Accountability in the Workplace." Xconomy, San-Francisco. May 2nd, 2014. http://www.xconomy.com/san-francisco/2014/05/02/cultivating-accountability-in-the-workplace/

Websites and Blogs

Ten Engaging Conversations, Changing Winds Adapted from "Building Trust and Credibility with Others." Copyright 1999 by Parlay International, Emeryville, CA.

"Professional Bull Riders." https://www.pbr.com/en/education/dictionary.aspx

Edberg, Henrik. "How to Take More Action; 9 Powerful Tips." Positivityblog.

"Concepts from Dan Crim." Richard Ivey School of Business

"7 Hidden Benefits of Process Mapping." Big Sky Associates.

Shook, Mike. "Seven Constraints to Business Growth." The Accelerence Blog.

Ehrenberg, David. "Envision New Markets." Early Growth Financial Services.

ABOUT THE AUTHOR

Bryan has been a corporate executive, business owner, and management consultant to the manufacturing industry since 1990. His expertise has assisted multi-million dollar companies become more profitable and to achieve their strategic growth objectives. His specialized approach of developing and executing business strategy is extremely effective and recognized.

Bryan held positions as Senior Executive, Business Unit Manager, V.P. Sales and Marketing, and National Sales Manager for Illinois Tool Works (ITW), a Fortune 200 Company. He has extensive experience in the manufacturing sector facilitating turnarounds achieving millions in increased revenues while realizing significant net margin improvements. Koala Corporation, one of the companies where he facilitated his specialized strategy, was recognized by Forbes as one of the Best 200 Small Companies in America.

Bryan received his bachelors degree from: Utah State University—Industrial Engineering and later attended the University of Michigan—Finance.